A PILGRIM'S HANDBOOK

DUBLIN DIOCESAN
JUBILEE COMMITTEE

A Pilgrim's Handbook

the columba press

First published in 1999 by
the columba press
55A Spruce Avenue, Stillorgan Industrial Park,
Blackrock, Co Dublin

Cover and design by Bill Bolger
Illustrations by Natalie Connolly, on pp 22, 82, 84, 86, 122
are taken from *Glendalough: A Celtic Pilgrimage*
by Michael Rodgers and Marcus Losack
(Columba Press, Dublin, 1996)
Illustrations on pp 16, 31, 34, 147, 153, 166
are by Emer O Boyle
Origination by The Columba Press
Printed in Ireland by Colour Books Ltd, Dublin

ISBN 1 85607 2770

Copyright permissions are listed on page 171

The logo on the back cover is copyright © 1999,
Dublin Diocesan Jubilee Committee.

Dublin Diocesan Jubilee Committee:
Bishop Raymond Field, Chairperson
Fr Pat O Donoghue, Co-ordinator of Resources
Editor: Fr Desmond Forristal, PP

A Pilgrim's Handbook is the collaborative work of the
Dublin Diocesan Jubilee Pilgrimage Sub-Committee
Bishop Martin Drennan: Chairperson
Fr Martin Clarke
Mrs Siobhán Corry
Sr Mairéad Flaherty
Mr Gerard Gallagher
Br Finian Gallagher
Sr Bríd Liston
Fr Michael Murray
Ms Eilís O Malley
Fr Seán O'Toole
Dean John Paterson
Fr Gerry Threadgold
Ms Fiona Walsh: Secretary.

CONTENTS

FOREWORD

by Archbishop Desmond Connell

When we travel on a pilgrimage we are going to meet Christ. That is what distinguishes a pilgrimage from other kinds of journey. A pilgrimage is a journey to a place of meeting with God. In that way it is an image of life itself. A pilgrimage clearly has meaning because it has a purpose that lights up the whole journey. Life too has a meaning once we realise that it is a journey to our meeting with God.

A pilgrimage has a very special character by the fact that we journey together, with times for prayer to keep the spirit of the pilgrimage alive in our hearts, with times for chatting and singing, for getting to know one another and enjoying the company. All this is an image of the pilgrimage of life in the communities of family and friendship and in caring for others, inspired by the words of Our Lord: Love one another as I have loved you (Jn 15:12).

In this book you will find prayers and reflections. They will help to nourish the life of God within you as you make your way towards the place where he is waitiing for you. May you walk in his ways, always knowing what is right and good.

✠ *Desmond Connell*

INTRODUCTION

by Bishop Martin Drennan
on behalf of the sub-committee

To prepare for the Jubilee Year 2000, the Archdiocese of Dublin established a central committee to ensure the co-ordination of celebrations for the year. Various sub-committees were established. The pilgrimage sub-committee has produced *A Pilgrim's Handbook* for anyone interested in organising, participating in or going on a pilgrimage. It is hoped that this book will help you, the reader, to be even more receptive to the peace and blessings that are available to you as you journey with God. It is this gracious God who meets us all on every step of our pilgrimage through life.

A number of people deserve special mention. Sr Bríd Liston FCJ co-ordinated most of the research and gathered many of the diverse resources such as poems, readings and prayers. Sincere thanks are extended to Fr Des Forristal who edited the final text. Also to Gerard Gallagher who did the final proof-reading with Sr Bríd and brought this wonderful book towards publication.

The committee wishes to acknowledge the encouragement and assistance offered by The Columba Press in bringing this book to publication. Final thanks are offered to Bishop Raymond Field, Chairperson of the Dublin Diocesan Jubilee Committee, for his support and affirmation in the work of this project as we prepare for Jubilee Year 2000.

✠ *Martin Drennan*

PART ONE

A PILGRIM PEOPLE
AD 2000 AND BEYOND

──────── Section 1 ────────

THE JUBILEE YEAR 2000 AD

The Jubilee Year in the Old Testament

The custom of the Jubilee Year began in Old Testament times. Every fiftieth year was celebrated as a Jubilee year. A ram's horn known as a yobel was blown to announce the year's beginning. The aim of the Jubilee year was to restore lost freedom. This was a response to two main situations: first, where land had been sold to pay debts, leaving the former owner in dire straits (land as family inheritance was vital for survival); second, where a person was sold into slavery to pay debts.

The laws of the Jubilee Year set out to put these situations right. They set out to prevent a situation developing where a family became landless and destitute. They also wanted to make sure that a permanent class of slaves did not develop. So, in the Jubilee Year people returned to their property and slaves were given their freedom. The cancelling of debts was part of the Jubilee obligations.

The Jubilee Year was a time to remember God as he who sets free, who grants liberty to all who are captive. It was what the prophet Isaiah calls a year of the Lord's favour.

Jesus –The Fulfilment of the Jubilee

All Old Testament Jubilee years find their fulfilment in Jesus who through his words and deeds ushers in a year of the Lord's favour. Jesus proclaims good news to the poor, brings freedom to all who are captive, sets free the

9

oppressed, gives new sight to the blind (cf. Mt 11:4-5). All of Jesus' activity is an expression of God's favour. Through Jesus' death and resurrection this liberation is offered in a definitive way and, through the Holy Spirit, that freedom is ongoing in the Christian community.

The Jubilee Year in the Christian Community

The Jubilee Year is a time when Christians rejoice in the saving presence of Jesus. They want all to know the freedom he brings, they want all to be able to celebrate justice as a reality in our world. The year of the Great Jubilee ought to be marked by insistence on the dignity of those who are deprived and the oppressed, by active work for economic and social justice. The aim is to create the conditions where everyone can share in the power of Christ's salvation.

For the church, the Jubilee is a year of remission of sins and of the punishments due to them, a year of reconciliation between disputing parties, a year of manifold conversions and of sacramental and extra-sacramental penance (*Tertio Millenio Adveniente*, 14). It is an invitation to experience in a personal way the generosity of God's mercy. Those who have met a generous God can afford to be generous. That is the spirit of the Great Jubilee Year 2000.

The Jubilee Year and the Church

In the course of history, the institution of the Jubilee has been enriched by signs which attest to the faith and foster the devotion of the Christian people. Pilgrimage, which is linked to the situation of people who readily describe life as a journey, is one of the greatest signs of these signs. Pope John Paul reminds us that:

> Sacred Scripture, for its part, often attests to the special significance of setting out to go to sacred places. There was a tradition that the Israelite go on pilgrimage to the city where the Arc of the Covenant was kept, or visit the shrine at Bethel (cf Jg 20:18), or the one at Shiloh where the prayer of Samuel's mother, Hannah, was heard (cf 1

Sam 1:3). Willingly subjecting himself to the law, Jesus too went with Mary and Joseph as a pilgrim to the holy city of Jerusalem (cf Lk 2:41). The history of the church is the living account of an unfinished pilgrimage. To journey to the city of Saints Peter and Paul, to the Holy Land, or to the old and new shrines dedicated to the Virgin Mary and the saints: this is the goal of countless members of the faithful who find nourishment for their devotion in this way.

Pilgrimages have always been a significant part of the life of the faithful, assuming different cultural forms in different ages. A pilgrimage evokes the believer's personal journey in the footsteps of the Redeemer: it is an exercise of practical asceticism, of repentance for human weakness, of constant vigilance over one's frailty, of interior preparation for a change of heart.

John Paul II
The Jubilee year 2000 – *Incarnationis Musterium*

Pilgrimage and the Jubilee Year

The Jubilee Year will see us celebrating our Christian heritage and traditions in many ways. One of the oldest traditions of Judeo–Christian religion is that of pilgrimage. So it is that people are encouraged to go on pilgrimage in groups of two, three or more, in parishes, schools and other groupings. The possibilities are endless and parishes may find themselves discovering a local pilgrimage for the first time. While for many people the Jubilee Year may be a first introduction to pilgrimage, hopefully it will not be their last. Pilgrimage is something we could build into all of our lives as a real and life-giving expression of our faith.

SACRED PLACES

Sacred places are the meeting points between heaven and earth.

Sacred Space – Sacred Place

Pilgrimage places are associated with holy people, with saints, with the presence of relics, and as the location of visions or healing events. The holy place is a geographical location where the membrane between this world and beyond is especially thin. The hopeful pilgrim seeks to meet with the holy as a way of bringing meaning to this life.

What is it that makes a place sacred or holy? We imagine space as something that surrounds us, through which we walk as we make our way through life. Space is given, we do not make it. By itself, it is emptiness, no more meaningful than the emptiness and void of Genesis 1:1: 'In the beginning God created the heavens and the earth. The earth was a formless void ... and God's spirit hovered over the water.'

Place gives us a sense of identity. When we meet someone for the first time our initial question is usually 'Where do you come from?' In normal everyday activities, we fill places with activity suitable to that place's character: a football game in a playing field, leisure walks through gardens, prayer and meditation in an oratory or church, religious rites at holy wells, monastic ruins or sacred forests. In our sacred buildings mere space is converted into place. A garden or a church, a mountain or a forest are places whose sacredness is recognised by groups who pray there. Because of the special nature of a place, people view it as their sacred place, not mere formless space. Elizabeth Jennings puts it simply in her poem 'Absence':

> I visited the place where we last met.
> Nothing has changed, the gardens were well-tended ...

There was no sign that anything had ended
And nothing to instruct me to forget.

It was because the place was just the same
That made your absence seem a savage force,
For under all the gentleness there came
An earthquake tremor: fountain, birds and grass
Were shaken by my thinking of your name.
Collected Poems. Carcanet Press 1986

The Spirit is Everywhere

All of the cosmos is sacred and holy. Tradition reminds us that some places are set apart and holy because of particular events. Moses' burning bush and the site of Jacob's dream are biblical examples of places held to be holy because of the experiences of Moses and Jacob. God already dwells there. Jacob puts it beautifully. After falling asleep on what he thought was God-forsaken terrain, he awakens to see the ladder connecting heaven and earth: 'Surely God is in this place. It is Beth El, "The House of God".' Gen 28:16-19.

God created the universe and God has given us the earth. As its stewards, it is not for us to ravage its rich resources for personal wants or view its natural beauty as tourists just passing through. God calls us to walk as pilgrims and to recognise a network of sacred sites that reveal all the earth as Beth El, 'The Place of God'.

In life we need to create sacred spaces to remind us of the holiness of all of creation. Buildings such as St Peter's in Rome, Hagia Sophia, or Chartres Cathedral are all sacred spaces where people can encounter God. In our locality, a church, a park or a quiet few moments in the sitting rooms of our houses can be sacred spaces which we all need to visit from time to time. In Ireland, pilgrimage sites such as Glendalough or Clonmacnoise are places of retreat, healing and new life.

Sacred places are passageways or thresholds which help us to look at life differently. They provide an environment for openness to the divine. The beauty, awe and stillness of a mountain, a lake shore or a secluded monastery can give the struggle and routine of everyday life a sense of peace and direction. Because Christianity depends so heavily on concrete events, not just on abstract ideas, the places where the most important events took place have, naturally, attracted the curiosity of many Christians. Over the centuries, places associated with Christianity from Israel to Rome to Glendalough have become holy places. Sacred space provides an environment for that which is spiritual in our lives to be nurtured, cultivated and harvested. Today, more than ever, we need to create a sacred space in our homes. This may be a sideboard or corner where we place signs and symbols that help open us to the spiritual side of our lives. For many this will be a crucifix or a holy picture. For others it may be a special drawing or a stone from a recent pilgrimage. It is this awareness of the sacred that opens us to the spiritual and a need to worship God in prayer.

Sacred Places – Places of Worship
Another reason for a place becoming sacred or holy is because of the human need to worship. A yearning for the divine deep within all of us calls us to make contact with a being, a source of life outside of ourselves and beyond our everyday experience. In the past, gods were asked to aid a hunt or provide rain for good growing conditions. The desire to pray, to reach out, draws people to special places associated with the divine. Monasteries, convents and churches are places of prayer and ritual. Places of particular beauty, monastic ruins, holy wells, shrines to Mary and the saints, holy mountains and sites vested with a presence of the divine, all call people to worship. By going on pilgrimage we are responding to the call of the inner journey of heart, soul and mind to be in the place associated with the divine. No matter what a person's faith, the longing for the divine is associated with prayer and ritual.

Ritual

Ritual is one of the most distinctive features of being human. The ritual of funeral arrangements recorded in megalithic burial places, the placing of flowers on a person's grave or place of death today, speak of our need to mark an occasion with some activity. Ritual is a conscious practical activity that expresses an inner desire of the heart and connects us to the mystery of life. It assures people that they are connected in some way to the 'other'. This ritual may be lighting a candle for someone ill, sending a card or calling to visit. Ritual, through symbols and the senses, gives participants an immediate experience of the interdependence of all. It is central to pilgrimage, as we try to insert our whole being, spirit and body, into the experience. A pilgrimage to a holy well is usually completed through the ritual of circling the well, of drinking the water, leaving an offering and praying. Every sacred place calls for its own ritual. This acknowledgement of its sacredness must be united with the needs and prayers of the people on pilgrimage.

Different Kinds of Sacred Places

There are three main kinds of sacred places in our world:
Places of inherent sacredness:
> Places with inherent natural qualities: The Grand Canyon, The Giant's Causeway.
> Places of the manifestation of a god or a spirit: Mount Sinai, Sliabh Mish.
> Places with energetic qualities or miracle healing properties: Chartres Cathedral, Lourdes, Knock, Sedona, Arizona.

Places of historical sacredness:
> Birth-place of a Religion or the Founder of a Religion: Bethlehem, Mecca, Lumbini.
> Birth, residence, death or burial place of a Holy person. A tomb or sarcophagus that may contain a body or part

of a body: Castledermot, St Laurence O'Toole; Christ Church Cathedral, heart of Laurence O'Toole; Mercy Convent, Baggot St, Catherine Mac Auley. St Kevin's Monastery, Glendalough.

Shrines where the Relic of a Saint is kept and in particular where the Blessed Sacrament is reserved: Matt Talbot's body, Sean McDermott Street, and all churches and oratories.

A holy well, or a nature area which has been dedicated to a saint and or given spiritual powers by tradition: St Bridget's Well, Clondalkin; Croagh Patrick and Lough Derg.

Places made sacred by artistic creations and personal or communal experiences:

Religious symbols or buildings by virtue of being created or built in one place rather than in another, can make a place holy.

By virtue of being in a particular place Christ Church Cathedral, the Garden of Remembrance, High Cross, Moone, Co Kildare.

By virtue of consecration or ritual: Graveyards, consecration of a new church.

By marking sites, which are special to us because of a personal or communal experience: The Phoenix Park at the time of the Pope's visit in 1979.

PILGRIMAGE: A JOURNEY IN FAITH IN SEARCH OF WHOLENESS

Going on pilgrimage without change of heart brings no reward.

What is a pilgrimage?

A pilgrimage is a journey to a holy place for religious motives. In life, our existence seems to prompt questions as to who we are, where we come from and where we are going to. So the very act of pilgrimage echoes questions that come to us from that deeper journey of the heart. What is the reason for my being? It is not a coincidence that many who go on pilgrimage are at a critical stage of life – transition from teenage years to adulthood, a mid-life point or at the start of retirement.

Becoming a Pilgrim

There is a pilgrim in each and everyone of us which is awakened gradually. The disposition to pilgrimage expresses itself from the moment of birth, through the different stages of life, venturing out and settling down, to the moment of death and rebirth. These pilgrimages take us along many pathways: the home, parish and area where we grow up; the roads, the city streets, the seas and skies we travel through and the places we visit, all make us pilgrims to one place or another.

Pilgrimage is not just travel to any place but to a place which in itself is seen to have significance. It is a journey to a holy place. But what is 'holy'? The experience of many pilgrims might be one of disappointment with the place itself. The pressing crowds and often the commercial exploitation of the pilgrim seem to many to take away from any sense of the holy. Yet, despite these external dimensions, a deep fascination with many of the holy places remains.

The Pilgrimage

Simply arriving at the place of the holy does not in itself describe pilgrimage. Although the destination is not without significance, the act of travelling is also part of the experience.

For the Christian, pilgrimage acts as a symbol for the Christian life. The people of God are sometimes described as a pilgrim people travelling to a destination that is beyond this world. The Christian life also comprises an individual pilgrimage. There are significant moments or places along the way, vantage points from which the journey can be surveyed. Its end is to be with Christ, to be changed and to be more like him. Pilgrims are often seeking to make progress in their broader Christian life by undertaking a journey. They are attempting to understand and advance their Christian life by symbolising the whole Christian Pilgrimage in a single communal event.

Some people describe themselves as pilgrims in relation to a particular quest, journey or difficult experience within their Christian life. Some who have worked in very difficult or missionary situations refer to their experience and work as a pilgrimage. Others use the term to describe their ecumenical journey or their work for peace or reconciliation.

Reasons for Going on Pilgrimage

Many of the major religions have pilgrimage as part of their tradition. There is no one answer as to why Christians go on pilgrimage. Reasons will vary according to place, time, the individual and the community. It is not just for the sake of visiting a place where certain historical or religious events took place. It is more than this.

Pilgrimage may involve a number of factors. These may include a specific belief, Christian hope, faith and the search for forgiveness. It may include a cure or prayer for a particular intention or request. People make the decision to go to a place where they are away from their family, friends and homes to venture into the unknown. Paul and many of the early Christians wanted to walk in the footsteps of Jesus.

Praying for a miracle, or a cure which is physical, emotional or psychological is a general reason to do a pilgrimage, especially to a shrine of a saint or a well which is reputed for miracles. For one it might be the realisation of a long-held dream, for others the death of a loved one. Some may have in mind the fulfilment of a pledge or a promise. Some might undertake the journey in gratitude for an answered prayer. Others are spurred by a wish to review the direction of their life.

Some pilgrimages were undertaken for their ascetic value. This meant leaving home and country for ever. Penitential pilgrimages were undertaken as a punishment for severe transgressions or simply to bring the body into submission. In the 11th and 12th centuries people began to go on pilgrimage in expiation for their sins which had filled them with guilt.

Gratitude for a favour received, or the hope of having a wish granted, were and are still good reasons for many to go on pilgrimage. Ultimately, personal salvation and to provide for the comfort and well-being of the soul is the deepest desire within pilgrims. Prayer, sacrifice, devotion and some physical discomfort all combine to give a pilgrim satisfaction and fulfilment with a sense of union with God.

The Steps We Take In Pilgrimage

The actions involved in pilgrimages reveal some steps that pilgrims take on their journey. They become a reflection of the life of faith as a whole:

departure reveals the decision of pilgrims to go forward to their destination and to be open to the spiritual wonder of their baptismal call;

walking leads them in solidarity with their sisters and brothers in the necessary preparation for a meeting with God;

the visit to the shrine invites them to listen to the word of God, to listen to where God is in their lives and to sacramental celebration of the turning points of their lives;
the return, in the end, reminds them of their own task in life, as witnesses of hope.

It is important that the steps or stations in a pilgrimage are marked along the way by acts of reflection or devotion. So it is that we set out on pilgrimage in each of our local situations and areas, according to our strengths and needs.

Pilgrims and Tourists

People are constantly on the move. Ease of travel was never so available to people as it is today. Is there a difference between pilgrims and tourists? At first sight, it may not be easy to tell them apart. However, it is possible to distinguish between those who travel merely to find something new to see, to hear, to touch but without any realisation of their need for conversion, and those who set out with a pilgrim's heart.

For the tourist, except in unusual cases, the journey is almost always not part of the experience but merely an inconvenience to be overcome. On the other hand, for pilgrims the journey is as important as the arrival. Often, too, a pilgrimage group may include the presence of some people who would not call themselves believers. For some of these, the journey is all-important and the arrival is almost incidental, if not disappointing.

To the pilgrim, the sacred place is alive, imbued with its own character, resonant with a message regarding the nature of reality itself. Pilgrims see sacred sites but they never master or change them. Instead they themselves are filled by the site's holiness, carried away by what the site conveys and they are changed by the call of the holy that is experienced deep within. Through the power of prayer, presence and penance the pilgrim comes to new life.

Tourists often have a need to know the facts, the data about a place and may fail to sense the spirit 'hovering'.

Similarly we need to read beyond the site markers and the historical data to sense the sacredness, the spirit of a place and so find the spirit within us and beyond. Only then are we truly pilgrims and in 'this sacred place'.

For the tourist the travelling bag can be a security factor, as within it can be packed everything which is indispensable and everything which might be useful – and more besides. The pilgrim, on the other hand, for each article he or she decides not to take with them gains a step in the process of liberation and personal freedom. We do not own the earth, air, water. These are for our safekeeping for each other and our descendants. It is this humility towards everything living and every place which contributes to transforming a person into a pilgrim.

The following poem from the 10th century clearly highlights the call of the pilgrim:

The Call of the Pilgrim

Time to me to prepare to pass from the shelter of habitation,
To journey as a pilgrim over the surface of the noble, lively
    sea.
Time to depart from the snares of the flesh, with all its guilt,
Time now to ruminate how I may find the great son of Mary.
Time to seek virtue, to trample upon the will with sorrow,
Time to reject vices, and to renounce the Demon.
Time to reproach the body, for of its crime it is putrid,
Time to rest after we have reached the place wherein we may
    shed our tears.
Time to talk of the last day, to separate from familiar faces …
Time to barter the transitory things for the country of the
    King of heaven.
Time to defy the ease of the little earthly world of a hundred
    pleasures,
Time to work at prayer, in adoration of the high King of
    angels.

But only a part of one year is wanting for my three score,
To remain under holy rule in one place it is time.
Those of my own age are not living, who were given to
    ardent devotion,
To desist from the course of great folly, in one place it is time.

From *Pilgrimage in Ireland* by Peter Harbison

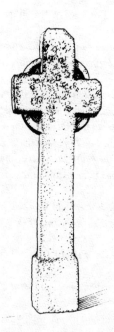

St Kevin's Cross,
Glendalough

EIGHT KEY ELEMENTS OF PILGRIMAGE

I have come that you may have life and have it to the full.
(Jn 10:10)

Pilgrimage is a universal phenomenon experienced by every human being either consciously or unconsciously. A pilgrimage may have an individual character to it for a pilgrim. Yet it always takes place in a communal setting. The following are eight key elements common to every pilgrimage experience.

1. Faith Expectancy
This 'expectancy' is based on an awareness, be it ever so faint, of a mystery in our lives greater than ourselves and towards which we are drawn. This awareness is heightened through prayer. Prayer can turn a tourist trip into a pilgrimage, a journey towards the fullness of life. A prayer and a blessing before the pilgrimage helps to create an openness to God in faith.

2. Openness to Growth
'Going on pilgrimage without change of heart brings little reward from God. For it is by practising virtue and not by mere motion of the feet that we are brought to heaven.' (*Book of Lismore*)

To grow is to 'change' and in the context of pilgrimage that change involves 'a change of heart'. Change involves effort, pain and penance, e.g. climbing Croagh Patrick or 'walking barefoot on the stones of Lough Derg'.

3. Community
The lone pilgrim does not exist. The tourist can choose their companions on the journey. The true pilgrim does not, but accepts and invites, tolerates and listens to all the fellow pilgrims along the way. God is not confined to specific 'holy' places. Any occasion, event, place or meeting

may become a truly 'holy' encounter. Very often God is revealed through others, e.g. the person who slowed down everything; friends from the neighbourhood.

4. A Prayerful Vigil
A silent space helps the pilgrim to face mystery on the journey. The power of mystery changes us. Being still helps the Spirit to work within us and bring about a change of heart. In quiet we discover the holy place within ourselves. 'If you do not find God at home, you will not find God in Rome.' A silent time by the river or a moment of contemplation in the ruins of the church.

5. A Ritual Expression
Inner healing and growth need to be expressed ritually, e.g. the leaving of a stone carried on the journey and taking a smoother one for the journey home. Change is the result of God's work within us. Ritual expression allows the pilgrim to make the occasion personal. A simple folk ritual created by the pilgrim group themselves involving symbol, dance or movement can be very effective.

6. A Votive Offering.
Just as the snake sheds its slough when the new skin has grown, so also we must leave behind that part of ourselves we have shed in the change towards healing and growth undergone. Something left behind, e.g. a coin in a holy well, a candle at the altar, a rag tied to a thorn bush, are signs of atonement. They are a symbol of regret for our refusal to change in the past, resulting in brokenness in ourselves and in others.

7. Celebration
Celebration is an essential part of pilgrimage as it is of life. It is both a celebration to mark the end of a hardship completed and a thanksgiving celebration for the new growth in Christ that has taken place within us. Untamed energy has been redeemed and channelled into growth. 'The mighty one has done great things for me' (Lk 1:49). What

we celebrate is what God has done for us, and in doing so we celebrate resurrection, for example, with a sing-song in the hotel or a picnic on the way home.

8. Commitment

'Short lived excessive piety is the work of the devil. The anvil of holiness is perseverance.' *(St Fursa)* Our growth towards wholeness and holiness must be ongoing and persevering. Change and growth must be maintained in the pilgrimage of everyday by a firm commitment to Jesus. When the pilgrimage is over we may return to the same place, yet we should not see it in the same way. We have climbed to a new height from which we can see new horizons and towards which we will set out again after a period of consolidation. Water from a Holy Well, the stone from Croagh Patrick, are all reminders to us of the resolution and the commitment we made on pilgrimage.

THE PRAYER OF THE PILGRIM

Lord make us the prophets of our times,
pilgrims not wayfarers.
May each day begin
With prayerful preparation
Opening our hearts to a spirit of loving repentance.
Make us aware, that although individuals we travel with
others
And help us to keep vigil with you in that holy place within
the heart.
May each event and meeting of the day be Eucharist
Leaving behind something of ourselves in Sacrifice.
So that we can celebrate and exult with joy,
Determined to allow Christ be reflected in us more and more
Thus heralding a new age of hope and joy and freedom.
Amen.

These Key Elements are developed in greater detail by Fr Frank Fahy in *Pilgrimage – Jubilee 2000 – A journey in faith in search of wholeness.*

PART TWO

GOING ON PILGRIMAGE

---------------------- Section 5 ----------------------

HOW TO ORGANISE A PILGRIMAGE

Practicalities

Many people and parishes would like to organise a pilgrimage but do not feel confident enough to do so. A pilgrimage has many aspects to its organisation and so the following is an outline to help parish groups, schools or individuals to plan a pilgrimage.

The best way to enjoy the special experience of pilgrimage is to prepare thoroughly for the journey. There are personal preparations which can be made by an individual on both a spiritual and practical level. This chapter will focus on the practical details of how to organise pilgrimage in general. The personal and communal reasons and aims for the pilgrimage in the first place need to be clear before the organisation begins. (See section 3)

1. How to organise a Pilgrimage

Define the aims of the organisation of the Pilgrimage:

• Be aware of the capability of the group selected.
• What type of pilgrimage do you wish to plan?
• Will the participants walk or be bussed to a destination?
• If they are walking check the distance carefully.
• What numbers do you expect?
• Will you be walking on roads or across the countryside?
• Will the pilgrimage walkers be physically fit?
• Are they a homogeneous group?
• Are they young, middle-aged, old or mixed?
• Can you anticipate their needs in advance of the
    pilgrimage?

Pilgrimages can be divided in terms of duration as follows:
1. A morning/afternoon pilgrimage.
2. A day-long pilgrimage.
3. A pilgrimage which includes one or more overnight stop-overs.
4. An overseas pilgrimage.

Pilgrimages can be organised for different age groups:
1. A general pilgrimage for all ages.
2. A pilgrimage for adults.
3. A youth/young adult pilgrimage.
4. A pilgrimage for children.

The pilgrimage should try to be open to those who are physically and mentally challenged because each person brings a unique gift to the group of pilgrims. The organisers of the pilgrimage may need to make special arrangements to accommodate the physically and mentally challenged who wish to participate.

2. Aims for organising a Pilgrimage

Be clear on the aims for organising a Pilgrimage once the destination and motivation are decided. The following is a sample of suggested aims:

• To allow all the Pilgrim walkers to participate in an environment in which they are respected and listened to without judgement, pressure or prejudice.
• To grow and develop as a community of Pilgrim walkers through faith sharing and witnessing to each other.
• For each of the Pilgrim walkers to take an active part in the organising and running of the walk where possible.
• To be prepared, as individuals, to participate at every level for responsibilities and tasks.
• To be aware of the importance of road safety and vigilant care (if walking on roads) and to respect other users of the road.
• To listen to those who have your own interest at heart.
• To enjoy the Pilgrimage walk.
• To appreciate and respect the environment through which the pilgrims walk.

3. Remote preparation

Most or all of the following points are relevant to whatever type of pilgrimage is organised:

Planning Committee.

Pilgrimage Manager.

Helpers (Appoint people in charge of food, back-up, liturgy, medical care, the route, etc.).

Local Contacts: Ensure they are willing to co-operate with the requirements of the Pilgrimage.

Advertising: Parish Bulletin/Local Radio/etc.

Participants: Invitation and Application Forms. Acceptance and Information.

Simple Pilgrimage Walk Booklet.

Cost.

Funding.

Fee for the pilgrimage.

Insurance (Make sure that the insurance covers all eventualities.)

Notification of the Garda of the date, the time and the route where appropriate.

Medical facilities: Qualified personnel - supplies: dressings / suncream / all First Aid needs. Plastic basins for sore feet!

Accommodation. (Where applicable) There are school halls, community centres or sports complexes which will be useful for cheap accommodation.

Food: Including special diets (vegetarians, vegans, special medical conditions).

Kitchen: Equipment and supplies. (Where applicable).

Toilet facilities on route.

Back-up personnel (water van, medical van, luggage van where necessary).

Transport: Before, during and after the pilgrimage.

Route: A map of the route is a great help.

Timetable of the pilgrimage. It is important to have a timetable. There are many who may not be able, for one reason or another, to walk in the pilgrimage but who would like to join the pilgrimage for the final gathering and liturgy.

Water van and water stops. Water containers plus cups.

Guidelines for road walking. (See below.)

Preparation calendar and pilgrimage details.

Liturgical needs: Bibles/hymn books/candles/vestments/symbols.

Permissions: Make sure that you have permission (in writing) to gain access to the pilgrimage destination. (The Office of Public Works, the local farmer, land owner.) Get permission from the relevant people when the pilgrimage travels across farmland.

4. What you need to bring

1. Every person is responsible for his/her own footwear. A strong pair of runners or boots which are comfortable, and well broken in are essential.
2. Waterproof clothing, including an over-trousers.
3. Spending money.
4. Suntan lotion and talcum powder.
5. Each person is responsible for bringing any medication that is needed.

For pilgrimages with over-night stops, all the above plus:

6. A rucksack, sleeping bag (and a ground mat if sleeping outdoors).
7. Enough socks, underwear, etc. (A thin pair of cotton socks inside larger ones is advisable).
8. Night clothes of some description along with a change of casual clothes for evenings.
9. Toiletries and towels.
10. Change of clothing.

For Pilgrimages which involve travel overseas:

11. Valid travel documents. (Check with Travel Agents).

5. On route

Make sure that the pilgrims who are walking do not have to carry any luggage as unnecessary weight increases the possibilities of blisters and sore feet, makes people irritable and gives the medical team unnecessary work.

If the pilgrimage involves walking on regular roads you can estimate their time of arrival and take note of the 'Guidelines for Walking on Roads' below. (Relatively fit pilgrims will walk at approximately 3.25 miles per hour.)

Aim for a water-stop every hour and a quarter if the weather is cool and stop every hour if the weather is hot. The stops will revive drooping spirits and will also give the slower participants a chance to catch up. It is a good idea to invite people after every water-stop to walk with someone they do not know. This helps people to mix. Questions for discussion on the pilgrimage can be given out at every water-stop.

It is more difficult to provide back-up for pilgrimages which go across countryside. Try to ensure that water-stops are available. Twisted ankles and pulled muscles may lead to people being physically carried to the nearest road!

6. Guidelines for the walk
The safety of the pilgrimage walkers is paramount.
On the road:

1. Appoint two front-markers and two back-markers. Issue them with luminous clothing plus a small red flag each. No one is allowed to go in front of the front-markers and no one is allowed to fall behind the back-markers. Obey their orders and the instructions of those on back-up at all times.
2. Walk no more than two abreast. Single file on bends and hills.
3. When you are told to walk in single file there are no exceptions.
4. Use pavements where they exist.
5. Where pavements do not exist, walk on the right hand side of the road facing on-coming traffic.
6. Cross the road at official crossing points. The back-up teams will alert pilgrims to dangerous crossings along the journey.
7. No personal stereos are allowed. They are dangerous and anti-social.

8. Inform the back-markers if someone stops for any reason (visit to toilet, shop, etc.). The back-markers must wait for the pilgrimage walker who has stopped for whatever reason.
9. Report any accidents or injuries immediately to the pilgrimage manager.
10. Mobile phones/walkie-talkies are helpful for key personnel along the route.

7. Follow-up after the Pilgrimage

One area which is often neglected is the follow-up after a pilgrimage. A bonding may take place among the participants of the pilgrimage and they may wish to come together to share their experiences after the pilgrimage. Obviously, the longer the pilgrimage is the closer the bonding of the participants becomes. This experience can be deepened when shared in a creative way sometime after the event.

Look for opportunities to channel the enthusiasm generated by the pilgrimage experience. It may be possible to develop an on-going process whereby the pilgrims become pro-active in their parish life. They can be encouraged to learn more about their Early Christian and Pre-Christian heritage.

PREPARING FOR THE JOURNEY:
THE PILGRIM'S PACK

Once you have set your mind and heart on a pilgrimage it is necessary to consider what you will take with you. The most important preparation for a pilgrimage is the faith, openness of mind and heart with which you begin a pilgrimage. However, you also need to consider other 'baggage' you take with you on the journey. The greater part of any pilgrimage will involve both transport and walking. It is important to be simple and frugal.

A pilgrim should be identified by their pack. The motto is 'travel light'. While many of the very practical points have been identified in the previous section, there is also the deeply symbolic aspect of what we take with us. In the past a pilgrim would always have a cloak, a pilgrim bag with some water, light food and immediate necessities and a walking staff. Each pilgrimage would also have a distinct pilgrim's emblem. This equipment has been given different meanings over the passing of time. The pilgrim and his or her pack is usually blessed by the local leader or presider before departure.

The Pilgrim's Emblem

The pilgrim's emblem is either given to the pilgrim on departure or awarded to the pilgrim as an acknowledgement that the destination had been reached. It can be made of different materials, e.g. wood or metal or cloth. It may be in the form of a cross, a medal, or a coloured piece of material, perhaps with something written on it. In the past this emblem was accorded great religious importance and a pilgrim was often buried with their pilgrims' emblem.

The Pilgrim Scarf

The pilgrim's scarf is a light piece of cloth which can be carried or worn by the pilgrim. It reminds one of the 'attire of love' which every pilgrim must wear. It also offers protection against wind and weather. It can be adapted to serve many needs such as being part of a prayer space, a table covering, or it might even be given to someone in greater need should the occasion arise.

The Hat

The hat is a symbol of prayer and detachment from the world and its ways and provides protection from the elements in all weathers. In some areas it can be a good marker to identify a group or individuals.

Food and drink

While both of these are very necessary, it is important to keep them simple and nourishing. Water, the wine of the gods, is the best drink of all and food bars that have all the nourishment needed in a compact pack.

The Shoes

The shoes or sandals are symbols of following in the footsteps of Jesus, the greatest of all pilgrims.

The Tent

The tent, which may be needed for some overnight pilgrimages, is a sign of simple living, the church as a tabernacle, a holy place, the house of God.

The Pilgrim's Handbook

The pilgrim's handbook is a valuable resource to have as part of any pilgrimage. It can offer some inspirational thoughts, prayers and reflections when the spirit is feeling a little tired or dry. A handbook can also give some initial information on particular places or routes as well as be a friendly companion for prayer and reflection.

The Rucksack

The bag should preferably be small because the pilgrim should discipline him or herself in order to manage with little. The fewer possessions the better when setting off on a Pilgrimage. Some traditions have it that the bag should be of leather for like the dead skin, the pilgrim should 'deaden' his/her desires and needs against hunger, thirst, adversity and difficulties. Today this is not very realistic but a bag of some kind can be a good reminder to us of the transience of life. The bag should not have a lock, because the pilgrim needs to be prepared to both give and receive.

The Walking Stick or Staff

The walking stick is representative of the staff of the Good Shepherd, Jesus. It is the pilgrim's strength, support and companion on the road ahead.

A PILGRIM JOURNEY:

Stops and Stations

In the Christian context we are all familiar with the word 'Station'. We speak of the Stations of the Cross, which are significant points along the way that Jesus travelled on his final pilgrimage. We speak of Station Masses in our neighbourhoods in the country where locals gather in a family home to share the Eucharist together.

On the journey to a holy place, a shrine, a well or a monastic settlement, the pilgrim route will have particular 'station points' at which the pilgrim stops. If there are no obvious station points along a pilgrimage route it is possible to create or adapt a point of significance for the pilgrimage. These station points serve a few purposes and have a variety of significance. Arrival at a station is usually a chance to pause and pray, perform a ritual and take a rest as the group grow in relationship with one another. Stations are important points for reflection and so pilgrims may need some time on their own to reflect on the questions of life, in addition to communal prayer and singing. Stations give the pilgrim group a chance to 'slow down the hares and speed up the tortoises'.

The following are examples of station points.

The Holy Well

Some people believe that all wells have their source in one great well within the earth. Wells are usually regarded as sacred places guarded by the feminine spirits. They are often seen as the entrances to the womb of the earth and places of fertility. As the water is the most important gift the earth provides and comes from deep within the earth it reminds us of God's presence within us. To visit a well can be a healing and calming experience and can help us get in touch with deep resources within ourselves. Many important stories in the Bible are centred around wells which were places where God was revealed and relationships were formed, e.g Moses to Zipporah (Ex 2:15-22), the Samaritan woman (Jn 4:6-30). Local areas have their own traditions and customs around holy wells. They are usually called after a saint, though there are some wells dedicated to Jesus.

High Cross or Carved Stone
Many high crosses or holy stones are picture stories from the Bible and the early traditions of the church. Stones are tabernacles of memory. They hold our history and are powerful aids to teaching and preaching. The high cross brings us in touch with the many generations who have gone before us and mark us with the sign of faith by their fidelity to the Good News. A cross or stones often marked sacred places or the boundaries of these holy areas.

Statues
Statues by their nature draw us straight to the person they represent. Statues are often seen on the roadside, in the church ground, at the top of a hill, or at a holy well. Some are very old and a little bit the worse for the weather. In some places people tend to leave some personal object by the statue in thanksgiving for graces they have received. In other cases pilgrims place intentions for their own or others' needs in the arms or at the foot of a statue.

Monastic or church ruins or present-day churches
These holy places can be read like a book of experiences which people have created together and with God. At the entrance to a church one becomes aware of the pilgrim's willingness to accept divisions; the door of the church represents progression from one world to another. The actual pilgrimage can be symbolised by crossing into the church, a journey between light and darkness, between the visible and the mystical. In wonder and excitement one can see

how the landscape continually changes from one sacred place to another.

Graveyard

None of us have to travel too far to find a cemetery. Many pilgrim routes have cemeteries along the way and so it is an important place to pause and reflect on life, death and resurrection. Regardless of whether we have family or friends buried there, a cemetery reminds us of our own mortality and that this too will be our final resting-place. Death is the only certainty of our lives after the present moment. To pause at a graveyard is to consider what special healing we may ask for or to remember those who are preparing for the final journey at this time.

River Bridges

Flowing water is a reminder to us of the constant change in life. Jesus was baptised in the river Jordan. Standing by a river can be a reminder of our own initiation into the Christian community. Our faith may have grown a little dry or weary over the years. Here we have a chance to commune again with all that nourishes us. The waters too have their own stories. The bridge, or stepping-stones may form a link from the past to our future. They may be a link for all those hopes and dreams that have not quite been fulfilled but for which we still long in the depths of our hearts.

Stone Mound

Of itself a stone heap may have little significance except to mark a point on the journey, as on the climb up Croagh Patrick. Some people bring stones to a particular place or gathering. Others take small stones home to remind them of their pilgrimage or the people they met along the way. It is this collection of stones that creates the mound which will of its nature change size over a season.

Mountains

Mountains have always drawn people to a sense of the divine. The height and loftiness of a mountain causes us to lift our eyes and hearts upwards and inwards towards God. When mountains are covered in mist and cloud we have an even greater sense of being enveloped by God. In most cases, it was the breadth of the view over the surrounding area, as this helps to provoke a sense of beauty and fertility of the earth, as with the megalithic tombs in Loughcrew. There are many sacred mountains that are places of pilgrimage, such as Croagh Patrick. Other mountains and hills have their own local folklore which make them sacred to the people of an area.

PILGRIMAGE AD 2000

Jubilee AD 2000 is a very privileged moment in history. During this year all people are invited and encouraged to 'go on pilgrimage'. The Jubilee Year is an opportunity for us to visit a holy place, near or far, and go on pilgrimage in small or large groups. The traditional and more organised pilgrimages to places like The Holy Land, Rome, Lourdes and Knock are central to the Jubilee Year. In addition, local parish/diocesan, youth and ecumenical pilgrimages are being highlighted.

National Pilgrimage Day: 21 May 2000

Pilgrimage has always been a characteristic of the living church and part of the Irish way of life. Today pilgrimage is becoming increasingly popular within the different church communities. To help us place pilgrimage at the centre of our Jubilee celebrations, Sunday 21 May has been designated National Pilgrimage Day for Ireland. People may choose to go as a parish group, neighbourhood group, as a family or with friends. A pilgrimage is an ideal opportunity for local Christian communities to come together since it is part of the tradition of all churches. As part of the preparation for this day, it is hoped that parishes, schools, local communities and families will have researched and re-dedicated local Christian Heritage sites. (See Section 9). These then could be the point of departure or return of a pilgrimage.

A Parish Pilgrimage

The following is a general outline of how a parish group might organise their pilgrimage on this day. Initially it is good to form a group of interested parties and across Christian churches. One parish could be the host towards which the other parishes or congregations would journey. Pilgrims could assemble in their own church or sacred place for a Gathering Liturgy, (see section 18) and be presented with the pilgrim's cross and pack.

The group would then walk along a previously prepared route stopping at designated 'station points' along the way. Section 18 in the book provides guidelines for prayers and ritual at station points. These could be places of Christian significance, i.e. a church ruin, high cross, a hospital, a river, or a holy well, etc. Individuals or groups could lead the prayer following a particular theme, at these stations.

The pilgrims would then gather at the host church or at a 'sacred place' at a pre-arranged time for a liturgy at 'The Journey's End'. (See section 18). This is a great opportunity for ecumenical sharing and for an opening up of the good news with many who may have drifted away from the church in recent time.

A celebration of the faith and unity of the community could then be celebrated by a buffet or picnic, contributions for which would have been given by all the participants before hand.

Contact: Jubilee Office, Clonliffe College, Dublin 9.
Tel/Fax: 01 8372069 e-mail: dublinjubileead2000@indigo.ie
website:www.dublin-jubilee.com

World Youth Day: August AD 2000

From 15-20 August 2000, probably the largest pilgrimage of the Jubilee Year will take place in Rome involving an expected audience of over two million young people. World Youth Day events have been a significant part of the pontificate of Pope John Paul II and have attracted millions of young people over the last twenty years in places such as Santiago de Compostela, Denver, Manila, Paris. The Jubilee World Youth Day in Rome in August 2000 is promising to be one of the most memorable to date. All young people are invited to attend.

All enquiries on World Youth Day can be directed to
Jubilee Office, CYC., Arran Quay, Dublin 7.
Tel: 01 8725055
e-mail: jubilee@cyc.ie   www.cyc.ie

European Ecumenical Pilgrimage AD 2000

Pilgrimage 2000 is an initiative taken by the European Co-ordinating Group for Mission and Renewal (ECG). Catholic, Protestant and Orthodox churches are represented. The aim is to promote a tracing of pilgrimages into the roots and development of Christianity in Europe, together with an awareness of new hope for Europe through the modern ecumenical movement.

Past, Present and Future

The purpose of this Pilgrimage is

Rediscovering the roots of Christian spirituality in Europe.

Expressing unity and reconciliation between the different churches and denominations because pilgrimages belong to our common heritage.

Visiting and discovering holy places where the presence of God and the witness of saints has been experienced for centuries.

Expressing the spirit of repentance, silence, prayer and praise.

Expressing a lifestyle of simplicity and solidarity with a community.

Receiving and giving hospitality with local congregations.

The missionary engagement of churches in today's society.

MILLENNIUM RESOLUTION

Let there be
Respect for the earth
Peace for its people
Love in our lives
Delight in the good
Forgiveness for past wrongs
And from now on new start.
[Churches Together in Britain and Ireland]

Pilgrimage AD 2000

Five places/areas and dates/periods have been identified by the Mission and Renewal Group, to form the highlights of the programme. They are in the shape of a cross, in the sequence south, north, west, and east, with a final centre point. The first is (Orthodox) Easter 2000, and the end is Pentecost 2001.

1. Thessaloniki, Greece. April 2000

Thessaloniki is a place of special significance because it is where St Paul first came to Europe on his missionary journey and to which he wrote a letter. It is also one of the most important cities of the first millennium. (The pilgrimage start is 30 April.)

2. Trondheim, Norway. July 2000

In 1020 King Olav Haraldon was killed in a battle at Stklestad, Trondheim. Following miracles he was declared a saint and is called the eternal king of Norway. His shrine has become a place of renewed pilgrimage, especially around 28/29 July.

3. St Andrews and Edinburgh, Scotland. Sept 2000

St Andrew is the patron saint of Scotland, and a place is named after him where his relics were said to have been brought in the 5th century. 90km south lies Edinburgh, Scotland's capital, with many historic links, from the experience of King David in 1128 on Holy Cross Day (14 September) creating Holyrood Abbey, to the Reformation (John Knox). As the place of the 1910 World Missionary Conference, it has added significance in the modern ecumenical movement.

4. Iasi, Romania. October 2000

The relics of St Parascheva are here, and the feast day is 14 October. This is a place of deeply rooted Orthodox spirituality and a place for reconciliation between east and west.

5. Prague, Czech Republic. June 2001

One of the most recognised voices for moral and spiritual renewal for Europe today is Vaclav Havel, through his spoken and written words. Prague is the ideal city where people can meet from east, west, north and south.

Participation and Expectation

Modern pilgrims are many kinds. A few might visit all these places (and others not highlighted but within the total framework), spending virtually the whole period in pilgrimage. Most will visit only one area, although some might try to make a particular link between two or more places as part of their pilgrimage.

Methods of travel will also vary, as will expectation of hospitality and accommodation, from the simple to the sophisticated. But some element of walking will be a feature for all.

Contact: Eilis O Malley, PDR Office,
The Red House, Clonliffe, Dublin 9.
Tel: 8360410 Fax: 8571990
e-mail: pdr@iol.ie

PART THREE

PILGRIMAGE PLACES AND TRADITIONS

———————————— Section 9 ————————————

CELEBRATION OF
LOCAL CHRISTIAN HERITAGE

Some sacred places and pilgrimages are already identified. The following are guidelines that a parish, school or community might find helpful in identifying local Christian heritage. Before taking on any task it is important to consult with the local Historical Society or Cultural Heritage Group to ensure that the new group is not crossing boundaries. It may be possible to have members of such organisations on your committee. Other suitable people are historians, school personnel, people who have a knowledge of the area and people with leadership or organisational skills.

A Christian Heritage Group in a parish could be responsible for:

Identifying and researching the local saint and holy place, be it a holy well, monastic or church ruin.

Making this information available to others in the area.

Setting up and caring for a sacred space related to the patron saint in the church or in the grounds.

Organising a pilgrimage from the parish to a local or national site.

Guidelines for a Christian Heritage Group

Identify the local saint of the area. Gather as much information as possible about the person. Sometimes this saint may also be associated with other parts of the country and so contact may need to be made to share information. Much of the data around saints is based on folklore and so it may be necessary to hear the stories of the local people.

In particular, note the legends associated with the saint. Has the name been used as a Christian name or for place names in the area? Are there townlands, monastic ruins or holy wells called after the saint? What is the form of veneration to the saint in the area today? Any prayers associated with the person?

Identify ancient ruins, monastic sites, round towers, high crosses, holy stones, etc in the area. Gather the information and see what in particular is relevant to the school or parish and to the area at large. How did it come to be built and when? How has the site been preserved? Is it accessible? When can the site be visited? What needs to be done to existing sites if they are within the care of the school or parish? This may involve a wider group of workers depending on the site and its needs. Contact may need to be made with the heritage society, *Dúchas*.

Holy wells are to be found in almost every parish in Ireland. Many have a clear story and tradition, others may need to be explored and developed. What are the stories, customs, patterns associated with them? What time of the year are they visited? What particular healing powers do they have?

Parish missionaries who have carried the word of God near and far are central to the Christian life of any community. It is important to focus on lay and religious people, of all Christian denominations, who have worked at home and abroad over the years right up to the present day. Who are they? Where did they come from and where did they go? What group did they belong to and who did they work with while sharing the Good News? What work did they do and how is it continuing today? Where are these people buried? What is it that we share today through the communion of all God's people, living and dead?

Parish/local photographs, artefacts, parish magazines, local historical societies or people with a particular interest in history over the years may be able to help form a valuable historical collection. Any events that took place relating to

Christianity over the years in the area, some happy and other more sad or divisive events, may need to be recorded as part of our journey in reconciliation. Old prayer books or books used for teaching religion can be a great sources of learning and appreciation of our past and present.

Prayers, poems, hymns and sayings are often unique to an area. Every area could collect and present a compendium of these that have any Christian connection with the area. It is important to do this before the older generations pass on. Children could be involved in building up these local collections by visiting some people.

Organise Local Celebration

Every parish or area will have its own time to celebrate the local saints or traditions. This will include prayers associated with local saint and tradition of the area. It may involve the young people through the schools or in the parish. Paintings, banners, icons, music and prayers are a good way of involving people.

Is there a Pattern Day, (a day of prayer, especially for the deceased from the parish around the feast of the patron saint), in the area?

A local pilgrimage of short duration would be a good way to gather the community into a celebration. It is important to keep the prayers simple, brief and accompanied with symbols and hymns that are easily accessible.

Create a 'Sacred Space' in Church or Grounds

The Jubilee Year is a good time to honour a saint or mark a time or event in an area. Creating a sacred space is a good way of gathering people and will involve local talent.

Most of the above will apply to parishes that have years of traditions behind them but new parishes can create their own traditions. The name of the parish will help give a focus for celebrations of a local Christian Heritage. The actual geographical area and the local History Society may give up some local traditions which will guide the direction of the parish.

Create a 'Sacred Space' in the Home

In recent times there has not been much attention given to a 'sacred space' in the home. For a family a sacred space can be created by having a special place for the Jubilee Candle and prayer card. At Christmas the crib could be the focus of prayer. In Advent and Lent the Trócaire boxes can serve as a reminder of the needs of others. During the year reminders of birth or death or the sacramental moments of the families lives can help keep the presence of God alive through symbols in the sacred space. This sign of God's presence in the home must be restored if we are to ensure prayer is experienced in the home.

THE SEVEN PILGRIMAGE ROADS

According to tradition there are many well known Pilgrimage Roads in Ireland. The seven roads that are better known and being restored at present are:

Tóchar Pádraig, Co Mayo
Tóchar Pádraig is the longest of all the surviving Irish pilgrimage roads. This is a pilgrim road from Ballintubber Abbey, via Aghagower, to Croagh Patrick. There are many styles and stone flags along the way as markers for the pilgrims. It is all on one level through boggy countryside. Aghagower has a Round Tower and a medieval church. In the centre of the village is Dabhach Phádraig, a circular 'bath' surrounded by a stone wall. Beside it is an ancient tree, the clay at the base of which is said to have curative powers. Also along the Tóchar is a raised altar stone in Lankill and a holy well dedicated to St Brendan.

The Saint's Road, Dingle Peninsula, Co Kerry
St Brendan's Way probably started initially from Ventry. Today the starting point is Baile Breac car park through fields and roads via Kilmalkeder, a 12th century church, to Mount Brandon. Close to the road is Gallarus Oratory, built between 800 and 1200 in fine masonry, without any obvious use of mortar. The modern pilgrim must only attempt the walk with good guidance and when the mountain is clear. Pilgrims walk this road throughout the summer but in particular on 16 May, the feast of St Brendan.

The Pilgrim's Way, Clonmacnoise, Co Offaly
The shortest of the pilgrim roads is the Pilgrim's Way. The way probably started at the Nun's Church leading towards the monastery and ending at the tomb of St Ciaran. Ten miles east-south east of Clonmacnoise is Lemanaghan, where there appears to be another short pilgrim road.

St Patrick's Way, Co Donegal

A pilgrimage road led from the village of Pettigo to Lough Derg and beside it, at Drumawark, was a round enclosure like a ring-fort, with a cross within. Pilgrims still visit Lough Derg in great numbers from May to August each year.

St Declan's Way, Co Waterford

An extensive road is reported from Ardmore to Lismore. This is almost the same as the present modern road. Ardmore stands sentinel over a fine sandy bay on the south east coast of Ireland. It boasts a Round Tower, St Declan's Cathedral, house and holy well.

Slí Chaoimhín, St Kevin's Way, Co Wicklow

This road brought pilgrims eastwards from Hollywood over the Wicklow Gap to Glendalough. There are several markers along the way, the most notable being a large granite Labyrinth stone, now in the National Museum. The labyrinth is known from the floors of the medieval French cathedrals, such as Chartres and Amiens. It was walked by penitents on their knees as an equivalent of a pilgrimage to the holy places; it was also called the Jerusalem Mile. (See Route 1 to Glendalough for details.)

Turas Cholmcille or St Columcille's Way, Co Donegal

Other than Derry, *(Doire Cholmcille),* one place which still bears the name of Colmcille is this beautiful secluded Glen in west Donegal. Here the saint is still venerated annually by a *Turas* (pattern) or pilgrimage, on his feast day 9 June, and on Sundays between the 9 June and 15 August. *Turas Cholmcille* is one of the few traditional *turasanna* still faithfully observed in Ireland and which seems to hold resolutely to the traditions which surround it. There are remnants of what may once have been a more extensive pilgrimage road through boggy terrain traversed after the eighth century. The *turas* has fifteen stations, some marked by early Christian standing stones at which certain prayers are said. The prayerfulness of the stations in this charming valley evoke more that anything the essence and the spirit of medieval pilgrimage in Ireland. The *turas* covers about three miles and takes about three to four hours.

THE SEVEN PILGRIMAGE ROADS

1. Turas Cholmcille/St Columcille's Way, Co Donegal
2. St Patrick's Way, Co Donegal
3. Tóchar Pádraig, Co Mayo
4. The Saint's Road, Co Kerry
5. The Pilgrim's Way, Co Offaly
6. St Declan's Way, Co Waterford
7. Slí Chaoimhín, St Kevin's Way, Co Wicklow

CHRISTIAN PILGRIMAGE PLACES IN IRELAND

Our confidence and belief in the future is strengthened by how we contemplate and celebrate our past. Visits to holy places – a ruined abbey, a holy well, a high cross – are moments when we re-enter our memory and retrieve the treasures of the past. These tabernacles of memory give us renewed faith, hope and love that inspires us towards our future. The possibilities for pilgrimage in Ireland are endless. There are many local pilgrim routes and it is best that these are experienced as much as possible. The main places of Christian pilgrimage in Ireland are:

ULSTER

Armagh, Co Armagh
Armagh can claim to be – after Rome – one of the oldest ecclesiastical capitals in Europe. It was here that St Patrick founded his first bishopric in 444/445. It still remains the primatial see of both the Roman Catholic and Anglican communities in Ireland. Like Rome it is a city of hills. On two of these hills the cathedrals of the two main Christian communities stand. The Church of Ireland Cathedral is the older of the two and it stands on the site of St Patrick's foundation.

Downpatrick, Co Down
The town got its present name because of the alleged discovery there in 1183 of the relics of Ireland's three great patron saints, Patrick, Brigid and Columba (or Colmcille). Part of the present Church of Ireland Cathedral dates back to the thirteenth century. St Patrick is said to have died at Saul, a few miles away (in 461?) at the site of his first church.

Lough Derg, Co Donegal
The small lake of Lough Derg in south-east Donegal was

the only Irish place of pilgrimage known throughout Europe during the Middle Ages. Its fame stemmed from a vision of purgatory which St Patrick is said to have seen in a cave on one of the lake's islands. The pilgrimage involves a three-day or one-day programme of penance and prayer. The austerity practised by the pilgrims is more reminiscent than most pilgrimages today of the harsh conditions experienced by their medieval counterparts.

Devenish, Co Fermanagh

The peaceful and wooded surroundings of Lower Lough Erne provide the setting for one of Northern Ireland's best preserved ancient monasteries. The island is not far from Enniskillen and is reachable from the shore by frequent local boat service. The monastery was founded in the 6th century by St Molaise, and his grave is presumably marked by the once stone-roofed 12th century church which bears his name. There is also a well preserved Round Tower. A second Round Tower was discovered during excavations in the 1970s. The remains also include the 13th century Teampull Mór and St Mary's Priory.

CONNAUGHT

Croagh Patrick, Westport, Co Mayo

Even in pre-Christian times, Croagh Patrick was already the centre of a joyful festival in honour of Lug, a god of the people of the time. The Christian church changed this into an annual pilgrimage on the same day in honour of St Patrick. Like Moses, he is said to have spent forty days upon the summit communing with God and interceding with him on behalf of the Irish people. Every year, pilgrims climb 'The Reek', as it is known locally, carrying a stick, like the staff of their medieval forebears, on the traditional day, the last Sunday in July. It is the most populous of all Irish pilgrimages. The happy atmosphere of the pilgrims, young and old, continues the festival atmosphere of the Early Christian gathering with which it started its life.

Ballintubber Abbey, Co Mayo

Baile Tobair Phádraig gets its name from a nearby holy well dedicated to St Patrick. It was also the starting place for pilgrims going on the Tóchar Pádraig. Known as 'the abbey which never died', it has remained as a place of worship for more than 750 years. The grounds of the Abbey and nearby Holy Island, have been landscaped to interpret scenes from the Bible and the life of Jesus.

Knock, Co Mayo

The small unassuming village of Knock in the plains of east Mayo is now one of the world's leading Marian shrines. Fifteen people, old and young, saw a vision at the south gable wall of the local parish church in the evening of 21 August, 1879. The figures of the vision were St Joseph, Our Lady, crowned, and St John the Evangelist, dressed as a bishop, as well as the lamb, the cross and angels above an altar. Since 1879 there has been a constant stream of pilgrims to Knock from all corners of Ireland and beyond.

Aran Islands, Co Galway

These three islands in Galway bay are the location of Ireland's first important monastery, founded at Killeany by St Enda near the end of the 5th century. Many of his disciples went on to found their own monasteries in Ireland. The most notable sites include Killeany itself, and Temple Brecan, both in Inis Mór, and St Kevin's Church on Inis Oirr, where the church is dug out of the sand annually to enable a pilgrimage to take place in early June.

Clonfert, Co Galway

The Church of Ireland Cathedral of Clonfert lies close to the banks of the Shannon. It is famous for its magnificent Romanesque doorway of c.1200, one of the most richly decorated church portals of medieval Ireland. The cathedral marks the burial-place of St Brendan, to whom the church is dedicated.

Kilmacduagh, Co Galway

Close to the border of counties Galway and Clare, Kilmacduagh stands almost in the shadow of the beautiful stony hills of the Burren. Its most characteristic feature is the Round Tower. Unusually, it leans two feet out of the perpendicular, like its famous counterpart at Pisa. Nearby stands the simple, roofless cathedral.

MUNSTER

Ennis, Co Clare

The Friary was built for the Franciscans around 1240. The long hall-like preachers' church draws all eyes towards the tall five-light east window. The dominant square tower was heightened in the 15th century and the cloister was partially rebuilt. At the foot of the tower is a carving of St Francis showing his stigmata.

Dysert O'Dea, Co Clare

Dysert O'Dea, four miles from Corofin, served as hermitage for St Tola, whose enshrined crosier (now in the National Museum) must have been an object of veneration for pilgrims. There is a Round Tower with a Romanesque doorway nestling close to it. Standing in a field to the east is a High Cross of the 12th century.

Killeedy, Co Limerick

Cill Íde is the site of St Ita's monastery of the 6th century. She was originally called Deirdre but her name was changed to Ita because of her thirst for God. She is known as the 'fostermother of the saints', her most famous saint being Brendan the Navigator. A famous poem about her suckling the infant Jesus, *Íosagán*, is attributed to her. Tradition records that she died in AD 650. Her feast day on the 15 January is a parish holiday.

Sceilg Mhichíl, Co Kerry

The great pinnacle of rock, Sceilg Mhichíl, the larger of

two Sceilg rocks, is the location of the finest preserved
early Christian monastery in Western Europe. It was founded
by a small group of dedicated monks in the 6th century.
The rock is located 8 miles off the south west Kerry coast.

Ballyvourney, Co Cork
Gobnait is one of the best loved local saints with much
local devotion. A medieval wooden statue is still venerated
in Ballyvourney and rounds are prayed at Cill Gobnatán.
Her feast on 11 February draws many pilgrims each year to
Ballyvourney.

Holy Cross Abbey, Co Tipperary
The abbey was founded in the 12th century and its relic of
the True Cross made it one of the most famous places of
pilgrimage in Ireland during the later Middle Ages.

LEINSTER

Clonmacnoise, Co Offaly
Clonmacnoise, the monastery founded by St Ciaran in the
6th century, has two Round Towers, one of which is incor-
porated into one of the six surviving churches. It also offers
two complete and other fragmented High Crosses. It is one
of the most popular places of pilgrimage in Ireland. In
medieval times, the centre of veneration was the tomb of
St Ciaran.

Graiguenamanagh, Co Kilkenny
The Cistercian Abbey, called *Vallis Sancti Salvatoris* (the
valley of the blessed Saviour), is better known as Duiske
Abbey. It was built in 1207. Today, following restoration, it
is one of the finest Catholic parish churches in the country
and one of the few medieval churches in Ireland where
Mass is still celebrated.

Jerpoint Abbey, Co Kilkenny
Though the church is now fragmented, it still preserves
the Romanesque pillars of the original 12th century structure and the fine medieval chancel.

St Canice's Cathedral, Kilkenny

The cathedral is dedicated to the founder of a monastery in the 6th century. Beside the cathedral stands the only surviving remnant of the monastery and a Round Tower, one of the few where one can still climb to the top.

Moone, Co Kildare

According to tradition, Moone monastery was founded by St Columba in the 6th century. It is now famous for its unique tall High Cross. It is noted for its beautiful evocative naive carvings found particularly at the base of the cross. There are also scenes from the Old and New Testaments, as well as others from the lives of the desert hermits, Paul and Anthony.

Kildare Town, Co Kildare and Foughart, Co Louth

Tradition records Brigid as co-founder of Kildare and gives her birth c.454 and death c.524. Brigid is also closely associated with Foughart and it is a place of pilgrimage for many years. Known as *Muire na nGael*, she is much associated with works of charity, compassion and healing. She was venerated as the patron of pilgrims and travellers during the Middle Ages. *Féile Bríde* on 1 February is a very important religious and cultural feast in Kildare and in Foughart.

Lady's Island, Co Wexford

A small area of land jutting out into the sea is a place dedicated to Mary, the mother of Jesus. It is a place of pilgrimage for thousands who honour Our Lady each year from the 15 August to 8 September and on the days leading up to the feast. The pilgrimage tradition has continued since the monastery was founded by the Augustinians in the thirteenth century. Pilgrims walk around the area reciting prayers and then wade barefoot through the water on the shore.

Kells, Co Meath

The town of Kells is famous for the Book of Kells in Trinity College, which bears its name and is said to have been kept here for some time. Surviving from an old monastery here are a Round Tower, and three High Crosses in the grounds of the church. Another cross, the Market's Cross was at a street junction in the town and is presently being restored. A notable feature is St Columb's House, which in reality is a stone roofed church building.

Monasterboice, Co Louth

Monasterboice gets its name from a monastery founded by a little known saint named Buite, who died in the 521. Its main attraction today is as the site of two of the most important old Irish High Crosses, probably of the 9th century. The crosses show a crucifixion scene, the last judgement, Old and New Testament scenes, as well as scenes from the life of the desert fathers, Paul and Anthony.

Drogheda, Co Louth

Drogheda is thirty miles north of Dublin. One of the best loved Irish martyrs is Oliver Plunkett. He was born at Loughcrew near Oldcastle of a noble family. He was ordained priest in 1654, represented the Irish Bishops in Rome and was appointed Archbishop of Armagh in 1669. He remained in Ireland during the persecutions which began in 1673. He was arrested in 1679, was tried in London and was executed for treason in Tyburn on 1 July 1681. He was canonised in 1975 and is honoured in St Peter's Church in West Street, Drogheda where his head is preserved and venerated in a special shrine.

There are many other places of pilgrimage known locally, e.g. Gouganebarra, West Cork, and Innismurray, Sligo bay. Pilgrimages have been happening in many of these areas for hundreds of years. Some pilgrimages are well established in an area, parish or diocese. Other pilgrimages may need to be revived.

Map of Christian Ireland

Derry

Glencolumcille
Donegal ● Lough Derg
Belfast

Inishmurray
Sligo ● Devenish
Armagh ●
Downpatrick

Foughart
Monasterboice
Knock
Kells ● Mellifont
Ballintubber
Croagh Patrick ● Drogheda

Clonmacnoise
Dublin
Galway
Clonfert
Kildare ●
Aran Islands
Glendalough
Kilmacduagh
Moone ●
Dysert O'Dea
Ennis
Limerick
Holycross ● Kilkenny
Graiguenamanagh
Cashel
Killeedy
Jerpoint
Waterford
Dingle
Lady's Island
Killarney
Skellig
Ballyvourney
Cork
Gouganebarra

● Main sites
▦ Main cities/towns

PILGRIMAGE PLACES IN EUROPE

To trace the origin of Christian pilgrimage we need to go back to about thirty years after the death of Jesus. At this time, Peter the apostle made his way from Jerusalem to Rome. His mission was to establish the Christian Church in the capital of the Roman Empire. By moving from Jerusalem to Rome, Peter was switching the focal point of Christianity from a Middle Eastern to a European setting. Because of constant and cruel persecution, the growth of the young church was slow. It was with the Emperor Constantine, and his conversion to Christianity in the fourth century, that the Christians could practice their faith in the open.

It was Constantine's mother, Helena who first highlighted the idea of making a journey or pilgrimage to a holy place. She set out for Jerusalem in search of the True Cross.

The monks in early Christian Ireland had a healthy reserve about pilgrimage. Unless the enterprise was motivated by the proper dispositions of repentance and conversion it would have no spiritual value:

To go to Rome is endless trouble, needless pain.
The God you seek there, unless you find at home,
You seek in vain.

In medieval Europe the first two centuries of the second millennium were known as the Golden Age of Pilgrimage. During these centuries and for many years later, thousands of shrines and churches throughout Christendom became a focal point where pilgrims of every social rank gathered to ask a favour, to seek a cure, or simply to pray.

Pilgrimage has always been a characteristic of the living church and is again regaining a more central role within the churches today. The first Christians called themselves 'the Way'. They followed the way of life not only symbolically, but went out into the world as an expression of their innermost conviction that they were following in the footsteps of Jesus.

The most famous places of pilgrimage in Europe are:

Iona, Scotland
Iona is one of the smaller islands of the Inner Hebrides off the west coast of Scotland. In AD 563 Columba, an Irish monk, founded a monastery on the Island. After his death, Iona remained the centre of the Northern Christian community until about 1200.

Walsingham, England
In the northern part of the East Anglian county of Norfolk are the two villages of Walsingham and Little Walsingham. The pilgrimage starts at the Roman Catholic Slipper Chapel in the village of Houghton St Giles. The focal point for most pilgrimages, Anglican and Roman, is the ruins of the priory built in the fourteenth century. In the village itself lies the Anglican Shrine built around the spot where the original Holy House of 1061 was thought to have been.

Canterbury, England
In the year AD 597, Augustine and a small band of monks landed on the south coast of England and founded their first monastery at Canterbury. From here the faith was taken to all parts of Anglo Saxon England. Lanfranc, the first Norman bishop, rebuilt the cathedral and secured the supremacy of the Archdiocese of Canterbury over York in 1072. The religious power of Canterbury caused the conflict between King Henry II and his archbishop, Thomas à Becket, whose death led to the great era of pilgrimages to Canterbury.

Chartres, France
In the Middle Ages a number of cathedrals were built all over Europe. They are monuments of their time and were signs of faith and symbols of faith in the good and dark times. Chartres, outside Paris, stands out as one of the

finest cathedrals of this age. Much of the sculpture work was a teaching tool to illustrate the stories and messages of the Bible. One of its most distinctive features is the labyrinth in the main aisle. To walk the labyrinth was seen as an acceptable form of pilgrimage for many who would never get to Jerusalem.

Lourdes, France
The town of Lourdes is the Christian churches' most famous modern place of pilgrimage. It is situated in the French Pyrenees in the south west of France. It was here that Mary appeared to Bernadette Soubirous on the 11 February, 1858. The Massabielle Grotto is the centre of pilgrimage where the sick and handicapped are the most important people.

Santiago de Compostella, Spain
According to tradition, the body of St James was miraculously conveyed to Northern Spain from the Holy Land. The cathedral dedicated to St James is the principal pilgrimage shrine in Spain since the Early Middle Ages. Pilgrimage to Compostella is as strong as ever today. There is a strong Irish connection with Compostella. St James' Gate in James' Street, Dublin, got its name because it was the gathering place for Irish pilgrims going to St James' shrine from the Early Middle Ages.

Fatima, Portugal
On the 13 May 1916, Mary appeared to three children in Fatima, 150km outside Lisbon. Since then, on the 13 of each month from May to October, pilgrims gather to commemorate the apparitions and their consequences.

Assisi, Italy
Assisi is situated in Umbria, known as the green area in the heart of Italy. Assisi's claim to fame is as the place associated with the life of St Francis. Since then, Assisi has attracted

Christian pilgrims from all over the world. While there are many religious festivals, the chief celebration is on 4 October, the feast of St Francis, patron of Italy.

Rome, Italy

Rome is situated on the west coast of Italy with a Mediterranean climate. Rome has played a central role in the political, cultural and religious history of Europe. It is as a place of persecution, of magnificent churches and a centre of leadership for the Roman Catholic Church that Christian people visit Rome in their thousands each year.

Czestochowa, Poland

Czestochowa is situated 290km south of Warsaw, southern Poland. The monastery of Jasna Gora, housing a picture of Our Lady which was discovered in 1382, is the central place of pilgrimage. Strengthened by legend, it has made Jasna Gora the centre of pilgrimage for nearly six centuries. On certain feast days in the summer months the town is transformed by a constant flow of pilgrims.

Holy Land, Israel

In the western Mediterranean, the Holy land is a small country only 35km in length and less than 100km across its widest point. As home to the world religions of Judaism and Christianity, the Holy Land has a history dating back to 3000 BC. The key figures and events in her history are: Abraham 2000 BC, Moses 1500 BC, David, 1000 BC, Exile 500 BC, Birth of Jesus 0, Byzantines AD 500, Crusaders AD 1000, Turks AD 1500, Modern AD 2000. It is all of this that makes it one of the greatest places of pilgrimage in the world.

MAP OF PILGRIMAGE PLACES IN EUROPE

1. Iona, Scotland
2. Walsingham, England
3. Canterbury, England
4. Chartres, France
5. Lourdes, France
6. Santiago de Compostella, Spain
7. Fatima, Portugal
8. Assisi, Italy
9. Rome, Italy
10. Czestochowa, Poland
11. The Holy Land, Israel
12. Thessaloniki, Greece
13. Throndheim, Norway
14. St Andrews and Edinburgh, Scotland
15. Iasi, Romania
16. Prague, Czech Republic
17. Eu, Normandy, France

PILGRIMAGE IN OTHER FAITHS

Pilgrimage in Judaism

The major practice is that of making the pilgrimage to Jerusalem as required in Deuteronomy 16:16. According to the Torah, all male Jews should go up to Jerusalem three times a year, on Passover, Shavu'ot, and Sullot (Ex 34:23).

In the days of the Temple, thousands of Jews from Israel and the diaspora converged on Jerusalem for the festivals to:

sojourn in the Temple courts,

to offer sacrifices, and

to prompt him to study Torah.

Even though the Temple was destroyed in 70 CE, pilgrimage continued even though it was a time of great sorrow for the Jewish people.

Jerusalem

The longing to be in Jerusalem endures to this day as a continuing theme in Jewish life, hence the phrase, 'Next year in Jerusalem!'

Since the Six Day War and the reunification of the city, the remaining wall of the Temple, The Wailing Wall, has become the centre of Jewish pilgrimage. The tradition of going up to Jerusalem for the pilgrim festivals has been resumed, particularly during the intermediate days of Sukkot. Since there is no Temple, there are no sacrifices performed during the pilgrimage at present.

Pilgrimage in Islam

Pilgrimage is one if the five religious practices enjoined upon Muslims as minimum practice. These practices are known as the five pillars of Islam.

The *Haje*, or pilgrimage to Mecca, is the one religious

practice amongst the five which is least incumbent upon the Muslim. The other four pillars of Islam are more present in the daily life cycle of the fervent Muslim.

The Pillars of Islam
1. The *Shahadah*
This is the witness of faith which makes a person a Muslim 'There is no God but Allah; and Muhammad is his prophet.'
2. The *Salat*
Formal prayers are conducted primarily as a public recognition of the sovereignty of God. This worship is formalised and includes standardised bodily positions such as bowing and prostration. The recitation of the *Shahadah* together with other formulae are also included. The worshippers face Mecca, a holy city in Saudi Arabia, and five times a day they perform the ritual.
3. The *Zakat* or Almsgiving
As the original prescriptions for the tax were not laid down in monetary terms, the practice today is considered as a general obligation to give money to charitable causes rather than as a law to be obeyed according to the details of a laid down pattern.
4. The *Sawm* or Fast
During the ninth month, Ramadan, Muslims abstain from all food and drink from sunrise to sunset. They do not abstain during sunset. The Islamic year is lunar, of twelve months, each of four weeks exactly. It is shorter than the solar year.
5. The *Haje* or Pilgrimage
Every Muslim is enjoined to going on pilgrimage to Mecca at least once in a lifetime. Obviously not everyone will be in a position to fulfil this religious practice. Mecca is a city sacred to Islam. It is the city of the prophet Muhammad. It is also the site of the pre-Islamic worship of Allah. Now however only Muslims are allowed to enter the sacred city. Pilgrims wear a distinctive two piece garment instead of

their regular clothes and all outward differences of race and rank and position are ironed out during this sacred time. They walk around the *Ka'bah* - the holy place where the first house of God on earth was established. The pilgrims are also participating with the angels and other creatures in their circling of the Divine Throne. Purity of intention is paramount during the pilgrimage. The pilgrim behaves as if he were a dead person having no control over his/her life and worldly activity. He/she concentrates upon his/her pilgrimage to God, prays, asks for forgiveness and devotes themselves to the mantra of the *Shahadah:* 'There is no God but God.'

There is the constant reflection on that Divine House in the Seventh Heaven, above and beyond which stands the glorified throne of God. The angels and the entire creation constantly rotate around this throne. The pilgrim then moves to the field of 'Arafat where Adam and *Hawwa'* (Eve) met after their expulsion from heaven and their prayer for forgiveness was accepted and a covenant between God and man agreed upon. To come to 'Arafat is to become fully conscious of that covenant and to remember that Allah alone is all in all. At this place the duality of purpose and action is reflected upon, the drive to secure wealth and position and the drive to serve the Lord. The great sin in Islam is *Shirk*, the association of anything with God. The pilgrim then goes to Muzdalifah to spend the night in prayer and meditation so as to establish within themselves the realisations achieved at 'Arafat. This is also called the place for the *Dhikr*, remembrance of the Divine Names.

The pilgrim then proceeds to Mina to throw stones at Satan and to sacrifice an animal in the name of God. Satan tried to deceive Abraham and Ishmael. The high point of the pilgrimage is the commemoration of the sacrifice carried out by Abraham of a ram instead of his son Ishma'il, as opposed to Isaac in the Bible account. The sacrifice of the most precious things of life for the cause of God is the final test of the pilgrim's surrender.

Pilgrimage in Hinduism

Pilgrimage is very important at two levels in Hinduism, which is the main religion in India.

The interior pilgrimage is expressed in the yogi who 'visits' the seven sacred cities while remaining still in a specific kind of meditation.

The exterior pilgrimage is obvious in the constant movement of people in every part of India, especially in the seven cities.

Major Sites

Prayaga, Gaya and Kasi are the major cities on the Ganges, with Kasi being the greatest. If a person makes a pilgrimage to Kasi and dies there, it means that the burden of karma and the necessity of rebirth are removed by Siva.

In India, place of pilgrimage are called *tirthas*, 'fords', and the pilgrimage is *tirtha-yatra*.

There are so many *tirthas* that they cannot be counted. In ways the whole of India is a place of pilgrimage, because the divine power is present in all places and pilgrimage evokes the divine.

In one of the earliest references to pilgrimage, the pilgrim is likened to a flower growing who rises above the dirt: all the sins fall away, slain by the labour of the journey.

Pilgrimage in Buddhism

The Buddha himself recommended the act of pilgrimage and it continues to be a very popular and central element in Buddhist spiritual practice. The four most important Buddhist pilgrimage places are connected with his life. The first is in Nepal and the other three in India: Lumbini where he was born; Sarnath where he first taught; Kushinagar where, at eighty, he passed away and most important of all, Bodhgaya. At Bodhgaya the Buddha attained his Enlightenment beneath the famous 'Bodhi Tree'. A descendant of the original tree still grows over a stone slab marking the spot where he sat in meditation and is the principal focus of devotion for Buddhist pilgrims from all over the world. Along with these four, many other places associated with the life of the Buddha, and of later figures in Buddhist spiritual history (bone fragments, personal possessions, etc.) have been distributed and enshrined in distant lands, and these places in turn give rise to pilgrimage. Indeed, places of pilgrimage in the Buddhist tradition are so numerous that it would be impossible to catalogue them all.

The characteristic Buddhist monument is the 'stupa', found wherever the Buddhist tradition has taken root. In shape it resembles an upturned bowl with a spire on top, often resting on a square base. Stupas range in size from small, portable versions to very large structures like artificial hills. They are usually solid objects, built around and protecting a central casket of relics, sacred texts, etc. In Asia, most of the major pilgrimage places contain many stupas, often of great antiquity. A large central stupa will sometimes be surrounded by many others of various heights, built wherever there was enough space. Praying pilgrims weave their way here and there around the ancient stones, not unlike a 'pattern day' gathering at a Christian holy place in Ireland.

Sometimes the focus of a pilgrimage centre will be an especially venerated image of the Buddha, or the stupa-tombs of eminent Buddhist saints. Natural features such as sacred mountains, lakes and springs with a place in the Buddhist history are also the goal of pilgrims. Probably the most important holy mountain in the Buddhist tradition is Kailas, in western Tibet. The rigours of the journey around Kailas are such that the pilgrim's route includes a cemetery, for those who succumbed to the altitude and the harsh climate along the path.

Pilgrimage implies a journey and, in Buddhist custom, this movement does not stop when the destination is reached. The most common physical expression of devotion is the act of circumambulation, of repeated walking around the object of one's pilgrimage. This is always done in a clockwise direction, keeping the focus on one's right. In areas of Tibetan influence, banks of prayer wheels often surround the central stupas and shrines, kept spinning by the outstretched hands of circling pilgrims. Rounds of full-length prostrations are also common as are visits to various monasteries and nunneries which cluster around the more important sites. Lamps are offered, patches of gold leaf rubbed on the mountains, and gifts given to the needy. The air is full of murmured invocations, incense, the chanting of the monastics and the flapping of prayer flags, all combining to produce an atmosphere of tranquil spiritual intensity.

Ideally, pilgrimage in the Buddhist tradition is one way of stepping out of the usual worldly routine for a time to involve the whole of one's being – body, speech and mind – in spiritual practice, reflecting on the example of the Buddha and other teachers, and strengthening one's connection to the good.

John O'Neill
Buddhist Centre, Dublin

PART FOUR

PILGRIMAGE IN DUBLIN DIOCESE

———————— Section 14 ————————

PILGRIMAGE SAINTS
ST KEVIN AND ST LAURENCE O'TOOLE

Kevin of Glendalough
Gleann Dá Locha, the Valley of the Two Lakes, is one of
the best known and loved early medieval Christian sites in
Ireland. Its founder and patron, Kevin or Coemgen/
Caoimhín, is one of our best known and loved saints. In
terms of re-discovering our Christian heritage and in
allowing it to inspire us on our journey into the third millennium of Christian times, Glendalough and Kevin offer
us a wonderful possibility of encounter with a vibrant and
rich tradition. The nearness of Glendalough to Dublin
and its hinterland brings all of this right to the doorstep of
a large portion of the nation's population. As we seek to
revisit the past in our attempts to renew ourselves for the
future, it can be seen how Glendalough and the tradition
Kevin represents could become such a wellspring for our
times. Kevin is said to have died either in AD 618 or 622.

Kevin and history
He was born into a family which belonged to the Dál Messe
Corb, a noble Leinster people. They lived in what is now
west Wicklow and had, in fact, been the ruling family of
Leinster at one time but were ousted towards the end of
the 5th century. During this time and up to Kevin's own
day, east Wicklow, the coastal area between the mountains
and the sea, would have been largely uninhabited.

Two Lives of Kevin in Latin and three in Irish come
down to us but, as with many of the lives of the saints, it is
difficult to know who Kevin really is. Much of the material

follows a familiar pattern and we must remember that the material in the lives has as much, if not more, to do with the later ambitions of Glendalough and its prestige as with providing a biography of the saint. Part of the purpose is also to provide reading material in the church or refectory. The establishment of the religious orders in Ireland brought great demands for lives of the Irish saints. The purpose of much of this material is edificatory and many of the saints themselves are lost in the mists of time. With regard to Kevin, we can get tantalising glimpses and these, linked with the extraordinary environment of Glendalough, allow us to get someway near to him and his spirit. Kevin or Coemgen is said to have been baptised by a St Crónán and to have gone to *Cell na Manach*, Killnamanagh, to become a monk (now a mile north of modern Tallaght, itself an important monastic centre in the medieval period).

St Kevin's Way

Having left Killnamanagh, Kevin set out to find his own desert place, his own hermitage. It is probable that he would have followed for the most part the route which is still known as *Slí Chaoimhín*, St Kevin's Way, from the west over the Wicklow Gap and into Glendalough. This route is now being restored as part of a national programme of restoration of some of the great medieval pilgrim routes for the year 2000 . In 1972, as part of the work by the ESB on Turlough Hill, a portion of St Kevin's way was excavated at the Wicklow Gap and this revealed the paved pathway. The route begins at Hollywood (the Wicklow one; this name always delights the American visitor!) where one can find a St Kevin's Bed, Chair and Cave. In the National Museum the Labyrinth or Hollywood Stone can be found. This came from Lockstown Hill west of Hollywood, and it has been suggested that this, too, was a marker on the pilgrim route. Labyrinths can be found traced on the floor in some of the great medieval cathedrals on the continent for the pilgrims to follow, mirroring the great pilgrim journeys to the holy places. Cross-slabs and other markers can also be still identified on the route to Glendalough today.

Kevin and Glendalough

On arrival in Glendalough Kevin chose the area of the upper lake and settled on the south side of the foot of that lake. The easiest approach is still by boat and the site is marked by the remains of *Teampull na Scellig* (Church of the Rock) and St Kevin's Bed. This is an artificial cave about thirty feet above the level of the lake and seems to have originally been a Bronze Age tomb. Kevin lived the life of a hermit there with an extraordinary closeness to nature – his companions were the animals and birds all around him. It is said that he lived as a hermit for seven years wearing only animal skins, sleeping on stones and eating very sparingly. It is also said, however, that 'the branches and leaves of the trees sang sweet songs to him, and heavenly music alleviated the severity of his life'. Stories are told of how an otter rescued his book when it fell into the lake, and of how one Lent a blackbird was able to build a nest and hatch her young in his outstretched hands as he prayed. There are many other wonderful stories also in the tradition.

The Monastic City

Disciples were soon attracted to him and it was probably after this that *Teampull na Scellig* was erected on a level site about twenty feet above the lake. There would probably have been huts for the monks also, but these were probably of wood, mud and straw and have long since gone. Over time the community would have expanded. This led to the establishment of a further settlement nearer the lake shore. Here can be found what is called Kevin's Cell and Reefert Church. Reefert probably comes from *Ríogh-Fheart,* a royal graveyard. Tradition has it that this place was blessed with earth from the tombs of the martyrs in Rome. It becomes one of the 'Romes' of Ireland, one of the most important burial places and places of pilgrimage. The church at Reefert seems to be of the 8th century but it probably replaces an earlier structure. It has also been suggested that the site would have been enclosed by a wall and that there were signs of other structures which have now disappeared. All this building and expansion would, no doubt, have bothered Kevin, who never really wanted to leave his hermit's life and seemed to have sought solitude and the life of a hermit whenever possible.

It is probable that Kevin and his community stayed (and died) around the upper lake and that the great monastic city at the lower lake comes later as the result of further expansion. The lives tell us that an angel told Kevin to move to this site but this is probably the lives' way of linking Kevin directly with the later monastery at the lower site. The 'monastic city' of Glendalough is hugely impressive. A visit to the model in the Visitors' Centre will give an idea of its extent and the prestige Glendalough must have enjoyed in later times. It is the focus of many of the visitors today and despite the numbers who come there, it still carries its own special atmosphere.

Glendalough: a sacred place

Glendalough is truly an extraordinary place, and just as one thinks one might bump into Francis around a street corner in Assisi today, a visit to Glendalough offers the same possibility – go into the woods, pause by the lakeshore, seek quiet among the monastic remains and you might just meet him. And even if you don't you will feel his presence and can join him in the search for quiet and a closeness to God which was his constant inspiration. It is wonderful to see that Glendalough is once again getting many visitors from abroad who come as pilgrims. It is one of the great pilgrim places of Europe.

Go gcumhdaí Dia thú, a oilithrigh,
agus go ndéana Caoimhín tú a threorú ar Chosán na Naomh.
May God protect you
and may Kevin guide you on the pathway of the saints.

St Kevin and The Blackbird

And then there was St Kevin and the blackbird.
The Saint is kneeling, arms stretched out, inside
His cell, but the cell is narrow, so

One turned-up palm is out the window, stiff
As a cross beam, when a blackbird lands
And lays in it and settled down to rest.

Kevin feels the warm eggs, the small breast, the tucked
Neat head and claws and, finding himself linked
Into the network of eternal life,

Is moved to pity: Now he must hold his hand
Like a branch out in the sun and rain for weeks
Until the young are hatched and fledged and flown.

And since the whole thing's imagined anyhow,
Imagine being Kevin. Which is he?
Self-forgetful or in agony all the time.

From the neck on out down through his hurting forearms?
Are his fingers sleeping? Does he still feel his knees?
Or has the shut-eye blank of underneath

Crept up through him? Is there distance in his head?
Alone and mirrored clear in love's deep river,
'To labour and not to seek reward', he prays,
A prayer his body makes entirely
For he has forgotten self, forgotten bird
And on the river bank forgotten the river's name.

Seamus Heaney, *The Spirit Level*.

Laurence O'Toole

The second great saint associated with Glendalough is St Laurence O'Toole, Lorcán Ó Tuathail in Irish. He was born in Castledermot, Co Kildare in 1128. He became Abbot of Glendalough in 1153 and Archbishop of Dublin in 1162. He died in Eu in Normandy on 14 November 1180 and was canonised in 1225. His eventful life can be summarised under eight headings.

Hostage

Laurence's father was Maurice O'Toole, King of Hy Murray. When Laurence was ten years old he was given as hostage to Dermot McMurrough, King of Leinster, who treated him with great harshness. The boy was sent in chains to a remote area where he was ill-housed, ill-clothed and ill-fed. For two years, the king's son learned what it was to experience real poverty and oppression.

Monk

After two years, Dermot was forced to release Laurence and send him to Glendalough monastery, where his father could reclaim him. When Maurice arrived, he found his son had fallen in love with the life of the monks and he gave him permission to join the community. Laurence was only 25 when he was elected Abbot, and he proved to be the greatest Abbot of Glendalough since Kevin, its founder. He encouraged learning, enlarged the cathedral, built the church known as Saviour's Priory and renewed monastic life by bringing in monks from the continent of Europe. He was unfailing in his care for the poor and sold the monastery treasures to feed famine victims.

Archbishop

In 1162 Laurence left Glendalough when the people of Dublin asked him to be their bishop. He became the first Archbishop of the city of Dublin. Many of the citizens were Danes and were no more than nominal Christians. He made it his duty to deepen their faith and help reform their lives. He brought Arroasian monks from France to form a monastery at the new Christ Church Cathedral and to reform the liturgy there. He himself became a member of their community. He continued his works of charity, especially towards the homeless children, whom he fed and housed in his own residence.

Contemplative

Laurence was a man of prayer. He rose in the early hours to sing the office with the other monks in the cathedral and often stayed on afterwards, deep in prayer. Then he would walk for a time in the graveyard, watching and praying over the city as it woke to another day. When his duties allowed him, he liked nothing better that to escape to Glendalough and spend a few days in solitude in the lakeside hermitage which could only be reached by boat.

Mediator

The Normans landed in Ireland in 1190. The following year they besieged Dublin under their leader, Strongbow. Laurence met Strongbow to arrange a peace but the Normans attacked while the talks were going on. They seized the city and began killing the citizens and looting their houses. Laurence saved the lives of many by the sheer force of his presence and he carried the bodies of others in his arms to be buried. In spite of many setbacks, he was to continue his efforts as peacemaker to the end of his life.

Traveller

For the last ten years of his life, Laurence was a constant traveller. He often visited England in his efforts to bring about peace between the two countries. Sea travel was hazardous and shipwrecks were common. More than once, his ship was caught in a violent storm and its safe arrival was attributed to the power of his prayer. Travellers believed that when he was on board, they had nothing to fear. His efforts were not entirely in vain. In 1175 he was one of the signers of the Treaty of Windsor between England's King Henry II and Ireland's High King, Roderick O'Connor.

Legate

Laurence led the six Irish bishops who attended the Third Latern Council in Rome in 1179. Pope Alexander III was so impressed that he appointed him Papal Legate to Ireland with the responsibility of reforming the Church in Ireland and defending it against attack. On his return, Laurence summoned a council of the Irish Church at Clonfert which took firm action against the abuses of the time. It was only his death that prevented him from completing his work of reformation.

Saint

Laurence left Dublin for the last time in the spring of 1180. His mission was to settle a dispute that had arisen between the Irish High King and the King of England. Henry II, the Man responsible for the murder of St Thomas à Becket, Archbishop of Canterbury, received him badly, treated him harshly and forbade him to return to Ireland. Then he went to visit his dominions in Normandy. Laurence followed him, sick and exhausted though he was. He died in the monastery at Eu, without having met the king. His tomb in Eu rapidly became a place of pilgrimage and many miracles were attributed to his intercession. He was canonised in 1225.

GLENDALOUGH: A PLACE OF PILGRIMAGE

Glendalough

Glendalough, the Valley of the Two Lakes, has a magic which is known, not only to thousands of Irish people, but to people from many different parts of the world. The Upper Lake at the western end of the valley, which runs from east to west, is much larger than the Lower Lake further east. The Gleneala is the river which tumbles from a majestic waterfall and cascades down into the western end of the Upper Lake. It flows through both lakes and then joins the Glendassan River. The Glendassan River comes down from Lough Nahanagan.

The valley of Glendalough and the surrounding districts continue to be home for many faithful Christians. There are parishes of both the Church of Ireland and Catholic communities in the area. The Catholic parish church of St Kevin is located just 2km from the monastic city on the left hand side of the road towards the village of Laragh. It is an unique McCarthy church, the first uncompromisingly true church of the old type erected in the Archdiocese of Dublin. It was built in 1841-51 by a people experiencing the hardships of famine Ireland and remains an expression of amazing faith in Divine Providence.

St Kevin's Catholic Church

The parish church of St Kevin is the focus of a new development to celebrate Jubilee AD 2000 known as *Suaimhneas Chaoimhín*. This place of prayer represents an integrated continuation of the spiritual richness of Glendalough. Here communal worship of God, the daily spiritual and pastoral life of the parish, and the prayer of pilgrims, are celebrated within the church. People seeking a prayerful retreat can avail of the use of one of the five *Cillíní* or Hermitages. *An Gáirdín*, a meditation garden, provides an open air, secluded, contemplative space.

Today, there is a real challenge in discovering the various churches, monuments and crosses scattered around the valley. There is a constant invitation to spend time at each sacred place and listen to the echoes of 'those who have gone before us'. In Glendalough, the reign of God unfolds in the architecture, art, song, words and drama. It is visible in the natural beauty that surrounds the pilgrim at every turn. Here we are made aware that the reality that is invisible is made visible. Through Jesus' life, death and resurrection, God was given a face in the world. The task of the living church in every period is, by words and deeds, to make visible the face of Jesus and to follow his example.

Pilgrimage to Glendalough

To be a traveller, or a pilgrim, is to have an open, inclusive attitude to life. The first Christian believers were called 'those who followed the way' (Apoc 9:2). To be a Christian believer today is still understood to be on the way. We must continually look to the future, dare to ask new questions, dare to meet all life's challenges and seek new truths. It means to be willing to be changed. Only then can we reach our decisions, expand our perspectives, and look towards the future.

When we stand in Glendalough we stand on holy ground. It is a meeting point between heaven and earth. Here we are momentarily lifted from this world into the world of the spirit which is filled with beauty, truth love and mystery. It is here that we can experience the narrow divide between our past and our future, giving us the courage to live the present moment with faith, hope and great love.

A pilgrimage to Glendalough begins with a visit to the parish church, the present place of worship of the local Christian community. The church enshrines very beautiful Icons of St Kevin and St Laurence. If a pilgrim is following Route 1, then it is best to visit St Kevin's parish church on the way home.

In all cases a visit to the Interpretative Centre is optional.

If groups wish to visit this centre it is possible to organise a group entrance fee. One interesting feature of the centre is the scale model of the Monastic City of Glendalough which illustrates how the monastery operated at the height of its glory.

To follow any of the routes it is best that someone in the group has a familiarity with *Glendalough, A Celtic Pilgrimage* by Micheal Rodgers and Marcus Losack. This book outlines a brief history of each station or church along the route as well as some thoughts for reflection.

The possibility of having local guides should be explored. In the absence of guides an appropriate tape could be made which would follow the specific route chosen. These tapes should include a little history of the sites, some traditional folklore, reflections and prayers. It is vitally important that the visiting group takes responsibility for its own pilgrimage and not over-burden the local parish of Glendalough.

Pilgrimage Routes

Route 1: St Kevin's Way, Slí Chaoimhín:
Pilgrimage from Hollywood to Glendalough
Distance: 10 miles approx.
This pilgrimage follows, in a general way, the old St Kevin's Road to Glendalough from the Wicklow Gap. The ancient paving of the pilgrimage road can be seen within two wooden enclosures at the Wicklow Gap. It is best that the pilgrims use transport from Station 1 to 5. The group could then walk from the Wicklow Gap to Glendalough.

Descriptions and reflections on these stations follow the outline of the four routes.

Key to the map:

1. Hollywood Church/Grounds
2. St Kevin's Statue, Hollywood
3. King's River and Bridge
4. Templeteenawn ... Roadside
5. The Wicklow Gap
6. The Healing Pool – Glendassan River
7. The Monastic City – The Cathedral
8. Reefert Church
9. Upper Lake Shore

Route 2. The Derrybawn Way
Distance: 3 miles approx.

This is the longest of the walks within Glendalough itself. After a visit to the parish church it is best to park your transport at the first car park near the Interpretative Centre. This route takes the pilgrim on a circular route and could take up to four or five hours.

Key to the map:
1. The Glenealo River
2. St Kevin's Well
3. St Saviours' Church
4. The Derrybawn Path
5. Poulanass Waterfall
6. Reefert Church
7. St Kevin's Cell
8. The Caher
9. The Upper Lake Shore
10. View of St Kevin's Bed
11. Gateway to the Monastic City
12. The Round Tower
13. St Kevin's Cross
14. The Cathedral

Reefert Church

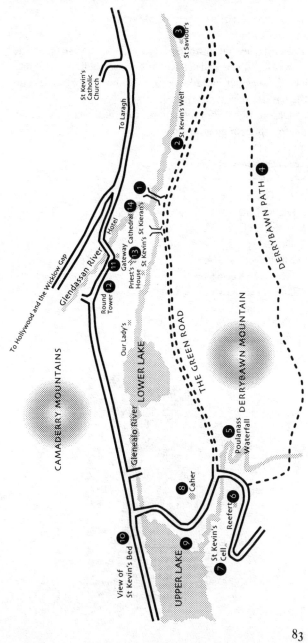

CAMADERRY MOUNTAINS

To Hollywood and the Wicklow Gap

To Laragh

St Kevin's Catholic Church

③ St Saviour's

② St Kevin's Well

①

④ DERRYBAWN PATH

Glendassan River

Hotel

⑭ Cathedral

⑬ Gateway
Priest's House St Kevin's St Kieran's

⑪

⑫ Round Tower

Our Lady's

Gleneálo River

LOWER LAKE

THE GREEN ROAD

DERRYBAWN MOUNTAIN

⑧ Caher

⑤ Poulanass Waterfall

⑩ View of St Kevin's Bed

⑨

UPPER LAKE

⑦ St Kevin's Cell

⑥ Reefert

83

Route 3. St Kevin's Desert and Monastery
Distance: 1 mile
This pilgrimage route takes in all the key sites in the
monastic village and St Kevin's desert beside the upper
lake. It does not include a hill walk and is more or less on
the flat. It takes about three hours.

Descriptions and reflections for these stations follow
the four pilgrimage routes.

Key to the map:
1. The Glenealo River
2. The Green Road
3. Reefert Church
4. St Kevin's Cell
5. The Caher
6. The Upper Lake Shore
7. View of St Kevin's Bed
8. Gateway to the Monastic City
9. The Round Tower
10. St Kevin's Cross
11. The Cathedral

The Gateway

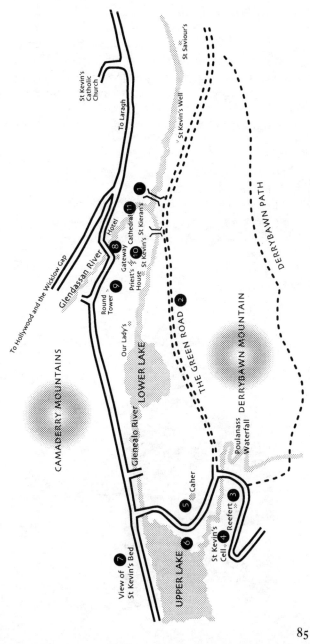

CAMADERRY MOUNTAINS

To Hollywood and the Wicklow Gap

Glendassan River

St Kevin's Catholic Church

To Laragh

St Saviour's

St Kevin's Well

DERRYBAWN PATH

Hotel

Gateway

Round Tower

Priest's House

Cathedral

St Kevin's

St Kieran's

Our Lady's

Glenealo River

LOWER LAKE

THE GREEN ROAD

DERRYBAWN MOUNTAIN

Poulanass Waterfall

Caher

Reefert

St Kevin's Cell

UPPER LAKE

View of St Kevin's Bed

1

11

8

10

9

2

5

4

3

6

7

Route 4. St Kevin's Monastery
Distance: Five hundred yards

This is the shortest of the pilgrimage routes in Glendalough. It takes in a visit to the main sites in the Monastic Village itself. This route is suitable for people who are not able to do too much walking. It takes about one hour to visit these sites.

Descriptions and reflections for each station follow this route.

Key to the map:
1. Gateway to the Monastic City
2. The Round Tower
3. St Kevin's Cross
4. The Priest's House
5. The Cathedral
6. St Kevin's Church
7. St Kieran's Church

St Kevin's Church

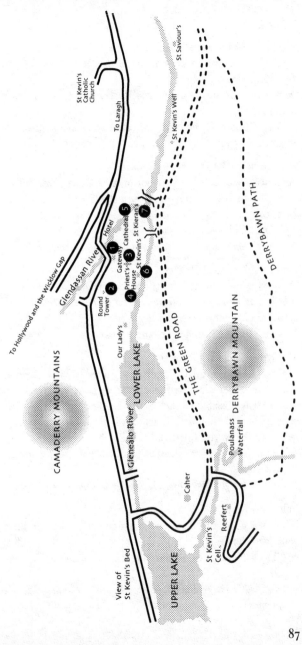

St Kevin's Catholic Church

St Saviour's

To Laragh

St Kevin's Well

DERRYBAWN PATH

Hotel

Glendassan River

5

7

1 Gateway

Cathedral

3

St Kevin's St Kieran's

2

Round Tower

4 Priest's House

6

To Hollywood and the Wicklow Gap

CAMADERRY MOUNTAINS

Our Lady's

LOWER LAKE

Glenealo River

THE GREEN ROAD

DERRYBAWN MOUNTAIN

Caher

Poulanass Waterfall

View of St Kevin's Bed

St Kevin's Cell

Reefert

UPPER LAKE

Hollywood Church/Car Park

Here the pilgrims gather and are blessed as they set out on their journey.

St Kevin: 'All our ancestors who walked this road now walk with us.'

Spirit of God help me to see and understand the burden, the baggage, I carry.

Statue of St Kevin, Hollywood

An undefined 'cave' at the foot of a cliff face, now with a statue of St Kevin, may have been the site of a subsidiary pilgrim's path at Hollywood.

Why did Kevin make the choices he did?

Spirit of God in the heart of Kevin and his followers.

King's River and Bridge

This river flow down from the Wicklow Gap.

The beauty of nature – refreshment for soul and body:

Spirit of God in the clear running water.

It is best to take transport to the next station.

Templeteenawn Church

This small ruin is off the main road on the left in Oakwood and is not accessible to the public without contact from Coilte. It is possible to park by the road and ponder on the significance of this little church. It is also a chance to stop, rest, and renew the spirit and relationships.

Where is God's Spirit when you see desolation and the life all around you?

From here to the Wicklow Gap is the last use of transport.

Wicklow Gap

This is a good place to have a sandwich before the long walk into the Glen!

'I lift up my eyes to the mountains, from where shall help come to me?'

Spirit of God in the wind – in my life – in my experiences on the journey.

The Healing Pool – Glendassan River

The poison from the mines – a threat to the river – my understanding of myself – my need for healing is threatened by the poison of a world with little acknowledgement evident of God's Spirit and yet, there is healing presence in this place.

The Glenealo River

Here we stop as we cross the flowing water of the river. The footbridge is a passage to the Green Road, drawing us into a sacred place in a world surrounded by nature. I am entering a sacred place. Here I ask for an open heart and a listening mind. These are the ways to good, and in walking them I come to new life and rest for the soul.

What is my purpose? What am I coming for? What do I really want from this pilgrimage?

St Kevin's Well

Water has always been a symbol of life and healing, even in the pre-Christian era. The well is symbolic of the well that is within our being. As the water from the well comes from deep within the earth, so does life within our being.

How is the well within me being cared for at this time?

St Saviour's Church

The walk through the wood to the church has a mystery all of its own. The latest and loveliest church in the valley, it is associated with St Laurence O'Toole, Abbot of Glendalough and Archbishop of Dublin. Built at a time of change in the church, it calls us to ponder on our need for change today. *Am I open to change? What am I holding on to?*

The Derrybawn Path

Return to the Green Road and take a left turn up the Derrybawn path. This is a good climb but it is rewarded with majestic views of the Upper Lake and the monastic city. *My sight and sound are gifts of God. Stop a while hold the moment. Smell the vegetation and feel the nature about. Am I able to stop and stare?*

The sound of the water draws us to:

Poulanass Waterfall

The water tumbling down is an image of the hectic rush of life today. The pool below the waterfall is a reminder of the need to slow down occasionally and rest awhile.

We all need a quiet place to survive the noise and the restless longings of our hearts. Where and when do I dip into the deep pools in my life?

St Kevin's Cell

This is a place where Kevin, the hermit, saint of Glendalough, prayed. This the place that still whispers 'Be still and know that I am God.' *Is it possible to be alone in the world today? Am I able to take time out and contemplate the journey, the places I have been and the places I am being called to?*

Reefert Church – Burial place of the Kings

This is probably where St Kevin was buried. It is a good place to reflect on the resurrection surrounded as it is by natural woodland, and the sound of flowing water. The early Christians where always looking for a place of resurrection and new life. We too need assurances that we are not alone. We are never abandoned. At the end of time we too will join the communion of saints and meet with God. *Take time to name those who have died and say a prayer for them.*

The Caher - The Homestead

Here are the remains of an old circular fort known as the Caher. Long ago there were dense forests all around the country. People lived constantly in danger, and could not protect themselves in isolation, so they would group together in homesteads such as this. Many of the early Christian prayers, called *loricas* or breastplates, expressed belief in God as the protector. They expressed the need for security and protection. Often before their prayers people drew a circle in the ground around them.

Circle me O God, keep hope within, despair without.
Circle me O God, keep peace within, keep turmoil without.
Circle me O God, keep strength within, keep weakness without.
What is my 'encircling prayer' today?

The Upper Lake
The experience of meeting God in all things has brought us to the place where the land meets the water. The expanse of lake is a reminder of the limits of our life. Beyond the lake the high ground is a reminder of the mystery of God. We are at the edge of life here by the lake. We thank God for the road we are travelling, for the beauty within and around us. We too leave something of ourselves in this place just as we take this moment in time in our memories. *What do I take with me as my most precious gift?*

St Kevin's Bed – View from the opposite side
St Kevin's Bed is a hermitage place inaccessible to us. The cave speaks of the courage and commitment of the early Irish saints to choose isolation. Here it is possible to sense the vulnerability of the inner self. Here we can reflect on our fears, dreams and ambitions. This is a place to observe and be silent and let ourselves be drawn closer to God. *What are my dreams? Where do I go for a quiet moment?*
Turning we walk back towards the monastic city.

Gateway to the Monastic City
It is good to pause outside the gateway looking through the archways to the passage inside. Here we are invited into a passage way, a place of transition to a sacred place beyond. This is the link between the sacred and the secular, the city of God and the city of the world. Touch the sanctuary cross incised on the slab on the right of the second arch. *Where are the transition places in my life? The places of sanctuary for myself and others?*

The Round Tower
The round tower stands guard over the ancient ruins. It is seven storeys high. It was a place of refuge, of sanctuary, of storage, and of rest. Perhaps it was built to give glory to God. Today it is a symbol of faith, determination, welcome and safety.
What does faith mean to me today? What values do I uphold and defend? What monuments am I leaving behind for future generations?

St Kevin's Cross

The cross is a symbol of salvation and hope. People gather around crosses and they are powerful aids for preaching and teaching. The high cross is a central part of our tradition and dots the Irish landscape. Our lives are full of small crosses, just by virtue of our humanity.
What crosses do I carry and how do I carry them?

The Cathedral

The stones of the cathedral church hold the memories of prayer and worship that has taken place in Glendalough over the centuries. The crosses and headstones within and without the cathedral are reminders of the passing of time. Stand for a while in silence catching echoes of the the voices of the years. *What would be the voice I would add just now? What would be my song? For what do I wish to give praise and thanksgiving?*

The Priest's House and the Cemetery

The name 'priest's house' comes from more recent times when local priests were buried there. The graves of two priests in particular who had reputations as healers were of special interest to visitors. Clay was taken from their graves and miracles were attributed to this clay. The cemetery reminds us of the many lives woven into the fabric of Glendalough. It also helps us to look at the transition from this world into the next. New graves call us to ponder on the death and destruction we still see around us to day, at home and abroad. *Pray for all priests and leaders in our church today.*

St Kevin's Church

St Kevin's Church is one of the most notable features of the monastic city and one of the seven churches in the glen. The original church was one room, with a vaulted ceiling and a stone roof. A distinctive feature of the church is the small round tower built into the west wall. This church is unique in style and a fitting memory to Kevin fifteen hundred years after it was built. The memory of Kevin calls us to look at how we too could take time out and reflect on our commitments in life.

St Kieran's Church

The original church was a nave and chancel but only a few meters of wall remain today. The church was probably dedicated to St Kieran because he was both a contemporary and a close friend of Kevin. Visiting this church gives us a chance to reflect on friendship in your life. *Who are the people that are most dear to you at this time? As a sign of friendship in your life you might like to place your hand on a stone or sign a cross on a stone with another stone, praying for your friends.*

The Green Road

The road to Kevin's desert links the old monastery to the hermitage near the upper lake. To walk the road is to make a transition from the community to a place of inner solitude. It is a chance to let go of my inner preoccupations and experience myself alone with God in the presence of creation. The trees are a connection between heaven and earth and remind us of the need to soar like the eagle to the sky but also to keep our feet firmly on the earth. The Lower Lake, *Loch na Peiste,* on our right, is a call to all of us to befriend the shadow within us. We need to know our strengths and weaknesses. *What are mine? How am I uniting my dreams and the daily reality of my life?*

At the end of the journey, wander alone or find a quiet corner in the city. Hold a memory of the pilgrimage. *How did I experience some of the elements of pilgrimage? What do I take home with me from this day? Thank God for the journey we have made, and for the beauty and mystery of Glendalough and the saints who lived here, known like Kevin and Lorcán, and many unknown who have left us with a rich and fruitful heritage.*

PILGRIMAGE IN THE CITY

A pilgrimage to holy places, that are filled with deep Christian symbolism and history, helps us to touch into our faith history. All these places have their own story to tell. In some cases, the building itself may have been the host to many a gathering over the centuries, or the place of worship of well known and not so well known people. In other cases the place is made holy by its association with a saint or holy person. All of you who have a knowledge and love for the city have your own 'sacred place' there, a place you visit to renew your souls, an oasis in the desert.

Preparing for a City Pilgrimage

As you set out on a walking pilgrimage in the city, it is important to recall some of the elements of pilgrimage: faith, openness to growth, community, prayer, ritual, offering of gifts, celebration and commitment. Because there are many distractions, it is good to set your mind and heart on the walk ahead. In a pilgrimage it is not the arrival that matters, but the journey along the way. As you walk from station to station, take time to 'look and listen' to the life that is about you. Devise rituals appropriate to the places visited. While you visit places of great historical significance, it is possible to be immersed in the life of the city, past and present. Take time to ponder on the people who prayed and worshipped in these sacred places over the years. As you walk along you will meet people of every age. Some people are shopping, talking or earning their living and oblivious to your presence. These people are in some ways reflections of ourselves. While telling their own story, they also reflect some of your own story back to you. Listen to them.

Christian Unity

All the pilgrimage routes are inclusive of the Christian denominations. While we might feel more at home in some places more than others, pilgrimage is an opportunity to join hands and pray with and for each other, at home and abroad. Visiting holy places is a reminder to us that the Good News is not just for ourselves, but something to be shared. What we have today, the faith we live, no matter how weak or strong, is something we have inherited from our parents and grandparents. Only God alone knows who or what will hold the faith in the generations to come. The new millennium must be invigorated with a serious, sustained and comprehensive effort to heal the divisions through the power of the Holy Spirit. This time is a graced opportunity to join with Jesus in our prayer and actions: 'Father, I pray that they may be one so that the world may believe that it is you who sent me.'

Pilgrimage Routes

The following pilgrimage walks outline routes that take three to four hours. They visit station points that are located close to each other. The first route covers an area that has a history going back to early Christian and medieval Dublin. In addition, it includes many holy places that date from the nineteenth century that are still places of worship and holiness today. Most of all, you walk through time in a living city and a living Christian community. Because this is not an historical tour of the city, details of the station points are not included. Many of the places visited have their own literature which can be read as you go along. Sometimes it is best not to get too involved with the facts of a place but rather let place speak for itself as you sense the sacredness of the place and the presence of God within and around you.

PILGRIMAGE IN THE CITY OF DUBLIN

The following are three pilgrimage routes in Dublin city centre. It takes about three hours to walk each one.

Route 1: West Inner City

This pilgrimage follows a route in west inner city Dublin. It includes some of the oldest buildings and holy places in the city. It takes in different Christian denominations and gives the pilgrim a chance to share their faith in a different environment. Some pilgrims may wish to end at the shrine of Our Lady of Dublin in Whitefriar Street. Others may wish to go on to The Church of Ireland church in Werburg Street.

Key to the map:

1. Christ Church Cathedral, High St.
2. Franciscan Church of the Immaculate Conception, 'Adam and Eve's', Merchant' Quay.
3. St Audoen's Church of Ireland and Catholic churches, High St. The Martyrs' Graveyard.
4. Church of St Augustine and St John the Baptist, Thomas St. 'John's Lane.'
5. St Catherine's, Church of Ireland, Thomas St.
6. St Catherine's Catholic Church and Grotto, Meath St.
7. Church of St Nicholas of Myra, Francis St.
8. St Patrick's Cathedral, Patrick's St.
9. Church ruins and Graveyard of St Kevin, Camden Row.
10. Church of Our Lady of Mount Carmel, Whitefriar St. Shrine of Our Lady of Dublin.

Also in this area:

Church of the Most Holy Trinity, Dublin Castle, Dame St.
St Werburgh's, Church of Ireland, Werburgh St.

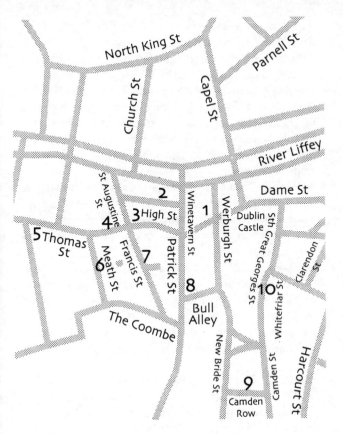

This pilgrimage walk begins at
Station 1. Christ Church Cathedral
This is one of the oldest churches in Dublin. Looking at the old walls of the church as you walk through the grounds you are carried back in time. Perhaps the sound of the bells are drawing you to prayer as they have done many others for centuries. Inside the church, sit for while at the back and take time to absorb the sacredness of the place, a place of worship for almost a millennium. When you are ready, move around by the side of the church on the left and visit the Lady Chapel, a feature in all medieval churches. The heart of St Laurence O'Toole is in the chapel for peace and reconciliation. A moment in front of the main altar and a visit to the crypt unite present and past in this holy of holies.

This church has many stories to tell. What are the stories that I remember from my childhood, told to me by the older people in my family? What have they passed on to me in my faith? What am I passing on to others through my faith?

As you leave the church, take a right down Wine Tavern St to the river Liffey. Crossing the street, the next station point is:

Station 2. The Franciscan Church of Adam and Eve on Merchant's Quay
The mission of the Franciscans is to bring Good News to the poor. The Franciscans have been in this part of Dublin since about 1232. In penal times the 'Adam and Eve' tavern in Cook St was the secret front for the location of the Franciscans. Two very special alcoves are dedicated to St Francis and St Anthony. A modern sculpture of St Clare reminds us of her spirit and enthusiasm for the Good News. The Franciscan Friars with their co-workers live out the call of Francis through care for the homeless, a *fáilte* for the many people who come to the door each day, as well as giving advice, counselling and social support for those suffering from additions.

Where in my life is there time and space for the less well off?

What justice issue do I have a passion about? In the spirit of St Francis, how am I protecting the environment to ensure that the generations after me will enjoy a city and country that is pleasant and peaceful?

> Make me a channel of your peace, where there is hatred let me sow love,
> Where there is injury, pardon, Lord, and where there is doubt, true faith in you.

Leave the church through the south door and turn right along Cook Street. Here you come face to face with the walls of the medieval city. Walk under the arch and climb the steps to:

Station 3. St Audoen's Church, Cornmarket and St Audoen's, High Street, The Martyrs' Graveyard

The present church, dedicated to St Audoen, is of Norman foundation (c. 1190) with further additions over the centuries. St Audoen's was in the heart of medieval Dublin.

The body of Blessed Francis Taylor is said to be buried somewhere near this church. The Catholic church on High Street was opened in 1846. The small park beside the churches is a good place to sit a while and ponder on the 'spaces' in life in the midst of a busy and hectic schedule. As you look north over the Liffey, ponder on the horizon of your life. *How far ahead do I look and where is Jesus? What grounds my faith and what are the dreams I carry in my heart?* In Thomas Street, walk west towards:

Station 4. Church of St Augustine and St John the Baptist, John's Lane

The Augustinians have been in Dublin since around 1280 and in John's Lane area for 300 years. Inside the church the statues of St Monica and her son St Augustine welcome the pilgrim. Straight away we are drawn to the bond that exists between mothers and their children. Age makes no difference. The story is old and ever new. Today as always parents pray for a wandering child or an adult gone astray.

Who do we remember today as we stand in this sacred place?
Who do we know to have wandered from family, friends, and
from God? On the right of the main altar is a shrine dedicated to Our Lady of Good Counsel. 'Mary, Mother of all
wisdom, pray for us.' To the left of the main altar is a
shrine to St Rita, an Augustinian nun who died in 1477.
Saint Rita has drawn many a praying heart to this church.
The stained-glass windows include images of Sts Patrick,
Brigid, Kevin and Laurence.

> *And love the high embowed roof, with antique pillars'*
> *massy proof,*
> *And storied windows richly sight, casting a dim religious*
> *light.* (Milton)

Back on Thomas Street turn right and walk west to:

Station 5. St Catherine's Church, Thomas St

References to St Catherine's parish can be found as far
back as the thirteenth century. The church was closed and
de-consecrated in 1967. It fell into disrepair but has been
re-opened and re-furbished and is now the centre for City
Outreach through Renewal and Evangelism, CORE.
Enriched by its history, St Catherine's is now developing as
a centre for worship, seminars, and furthering social outreach work in the city. CORE is a small but growing community and reflects a changing city and nation both in its
age profile and in its cross denominational and cross community involvement. It forms a bridge, reconciling our past
and present to enrich our future.

> *How do I experience outreach and reconciliation in my life?*
> *What are the lines or the barriers I have to cross in life? How*
> *were peoples lives changed because Jesus reached out to them?*
> *Who is caring for the young adult faith in my parish community?*

On Thomas Street, turn right and walk back east to Meath St.
Along the way you will pass the busy market stands of the street
traders. Pause and have a word with them. All human life is here.

Station 6. St Catherine's Church, Meath St

A shrine to St Catherine of Alexandria is said to have existed in or about Meath St from Danish times. This church, in the heart of the Liberties, was built with the weekly pennies of the poor. Today the church is administered by the Augustinians. The vision statement of St Catherine's parish gives us an insight into this thriving community. 'We are ordinary people wishing to create a parish where all feel welcomed and valued.' The presence of old and young gives a real sense of this welcome in walking around the church. Right outside, the busy street is teeming with life. A Grotto to Our Lady, hidden beside the church, is a place of prayer for the passer-by. *What is the bond that unites my work and prayer? Am I able to slip quietly into a place of prayer from time to time in my busy week?*

In Meath St walk left outside the church door and go south, pass Liberty Market as far as Carmen's Hall Street. Walk east towards:

Station 7. Church of Nicholas of Myra, Francis St

St Nicholas Church is built on the site of the first Franciscan church in 1235. There have been many churches since then, the present one dating from 1834. On entering the church one's eyes are drawn immediately to the altar and the decorated ceiling where there are paintings of four early fathers of the church, St Gregory the Great, St Jerome, St Ambrose and St Augustine. Another design on the ceiling recalls the foundation of the Legion of Mary in the Parish in 1921. This church was the old cathedral church of the Catholic community of the diocese.

Do I belong to any group or community where I share my faith and the faith of others? How do I receive and support the good work and outreach done by many who belong to social care and faith sharing groups around me? Do I give regular time to reading the word of God?

Outside the gates of the church, walk left, going south again to Hanover Lane. Turn left and walk under the arch to Patrick Street. Turn right and there before you is:

Station 8. St Patrick's Cathedral

St Patrick's Cathedral stands on the oldest Christian site in Dublin where it is said the saint baptised converts to the Christian faith in a well beside the building. A church to St Patrick has stood here since AD 450. In 1191 that old church was replaced by the present building, the largest church in Ireland. The interior of the church speaks for itself. Take time to ponder and be still. Remember the call of baptism and the gift of belonging to a Christian community. Walk the centuries with the stones and monuments, tabernacles of memory. Reflect again on the Prayer of St Patrick.

> Christ be beside me,
> Christ be before me,
> King of my heart.

Outside the Cathedral, turn left and walk along St Patrick's Close, towards Kevin Street. Take a right along New Bride Street as far as Camden Row. On the left beyond the College of Technology is:

Station 9. The Church and Graveyard of St Kevin

This is a real oasis in the city and now more a park than a graveyard. The body of Blessed Dermot O'Hurley is said to buried in a secret grave in the church. Dermot was a martyr for his Christian beliefs and is a witness to the faith of many people of his time when persecution for belief in all Christian denominations was happening throughout Europe. There is also a monument in the park to Fr John Austin, a Jesuit priest, who worked tirelessly for the people of the city. *How do I witness to my Christian faith today? Who are the people that are persecuted, excluded, judged in our society today? How do I welcome the stranger in my heart and in my everyday living?*

Back onto Camden Row, turn left and left again on Camden Street. Walk as far as:

Station 10. Church of Our Lady of Mount Carmel, Whitefriar St

The present church, built in 1825, stands on the original site acquired by the Carmelites around 1280. The foyer tells the story of the Carmelites in words and pictures. It gives a global sense of the church that we belong to and of the story of one group of religious over the centuries. There is, one might say, something for everybody in this church. There are several statues of the saints, notably, St Jude, patron of hopeless cases, St Thérèse, patron of the missions, St Albert, healer of all illness and St Valentine, the patron of love and romance! An oak statue of Our Lady of Dublin is placed above an altar on the right of the main entrance. This is a fifteenth-century statue of Our Lady and the child Jesus. It is called the Black Madonna because its tough oak was stained during the reformation when bright colours were forbidden in churches. It presides over the city as a sign of Mary's protection for her beloved children who gather in faith.

> *O mother of mercy, I place in the protection of your blessed hands*
> *my going out and my coming in, my lying down and my rising,*
> *the sight of my eyes, the touch of my hands, the speech of my mouth,*
> *the hearing of my ears, so that they may be pleasing*
> *to your beloved Son, Jesus. Amen.*

This is a good place to end the pilgrimage, but some may want to continue on Camden Street, walk left towards Dame Street. Turn left towards Dublin Castle. In the grounds off the main square is:

Station 11. The Church of the Most Holy Trinity

The Church of the Most Holy Trinity was once known as the Chapel Royal and was the chapel of the Viceroys. This is a church where history and politics meet and could be said to be truly an ecumenical gathering place of worship. The exterior decorations include some eighty six carved heads of English monarchs, mixed with Our Lady, Dean Swift, St Peter and Brian Boru. In 1943 the church became a Catholic Garrison Church. Today it is no longer a place of worship but a museum. *What has happened to the many 'holy places and spaces' in my life? Has my life become secularised and a show-piece rather that a dwelling place of God?*

Going out the main gates of the Castle turn left onto Castle Street. Bear left on to Werburgh Street. A few yards down on the left is:

Station 12. St Werburgh's Church of Ireland Church

St Werburgh's Church is one of the oldest in the city. Beneath the church are several vaults containing the remains of many famous people. Today the church is known for its charismatic mission and outreach.

Pilgrimage End

At the end of the pilgrimage it is good to take time to share some reflections of the pilgrimage.

How did I experience some of the eight elements of pilgrimage? What place stood out for me as special? What will I take away with me from this walk? What are the stories that stay with me? What one grace do I feel I have received and what is my prayer for the year ahead? In what new way has the face of God been revealed to me? What do I want to share with others from this pilgrimage?

The Liturgy section offers prayers for the end of a pilgrimage as you return home.

Route 2: East Inner City

Key to map overleaf:
1. St Stephen's Green
2. University Church, Stephen's Green
3. Unitarian Church, Stephen's Green
4. Carmelite Church, Clarendon St
5. St Anne's Church, Dawson St
6. Early Christian Art, National Museum, Kildare St
7. Huguenot Graveyard, Merrion Row
8. *The Flight into Egypt* (Rembrandt), *The Taking of Christ* (Carravaggio), National Art Gallery
9. Archbishop Ryan Park, Merrion Square
10. St Andrew's Church, Westland Row
11. *Book of Kells*, Trinity College

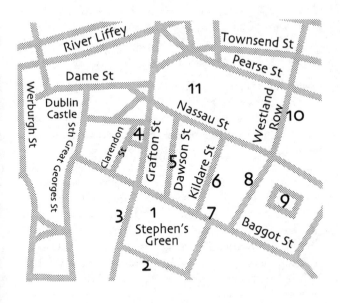

This pilgrimage walk begins at
Station 1. St Stephen's Green
St Stephen's Green is like a secret garden that is waiting to be explored. It includes a scented garden, a children's playground and numerous statues and memorials. Walk about the garden and let the senses speak to you. Listen to the sounds in the air: children playing, birds singing, water flowing and let their message speak. Enjoy the colour all about, the flowers, trees, the clothing of people who are resting and walking. Smell the scents of the garden and of the city. Let the memorials speak to you and tell their story. Feel the material from which they are made and the crafts of people who have created such beauty all around us.

Everybody has her/his own secret garden in life. Enjoy the moment and the gift of this day. Ponder on what grace you feel you most need at this time as you feed the ducks. *What gift does God want to give you these days? Is your heart open to receive what life is offering you right now?*

Leave The Green by the south west and cross to the south side of the square to:

Station 2. University Church
of Our Lady Seat of Wisdom
The unattractive red brick exterior and the large gateway-like entrance hardly prepare one for the very beautiful little church within. Cardinal Newman's idea was to have a church in the manner of a Roman basilica. Walk up the main isle to the Lady Chapel on the left of the sanctuary and stay with the stillness of the church in the centre of the city. As you leave take particular note of the ceiling decoration and the use of Irish marble in the church. Since the church has been associated with University College Dublin, ponder on the whole area of learning in you life. *Where have been the places that have influenced me and who were the people who opened my mind to the possibilities of education? What skill or learning have I received that I want to share and pass on to others? How does the gospel speak in our education system?*

Walk west on to the west side of the square and visit:

Station 3. The Unitarian Church

The congregation now worshipping in this church can trace its descent back to the very first congregation of Protestant Dissenters in Dublin during the reign of Elizabeth 1 of England. In the early years of the eighteenth century, liberal theological thought was to be found in many dissenting congregations. This congregation thought of itself as distinctively Unitarian. A visit within the church calls you to pray for unity. Ponder on the many wars and the great human suffering caused by religious divisions and fear.

Who do I want to remember as I look through the beautiful stained glass? In particular remember people who have stood up for their religious beliefs in Europe.

Back on the Green walk down Grafton St, taking the second left to:

Station 4. St Teresa's Church, Clarendon St

While you enter the church by the side aisle, it is possible to get a sense of what this church means to 'shoppers' of Dublin. Straight away one is drawn to the quiet prayer of the people, or to the strong responses given for a weekday or Sunday Eucharist. The Lady Chapel is a place of quiet prayer as are many of the other alcoves hosting statues of St Teresa, the Child of Prague, St Joseph and the Sacred Heart. This is a very devotional church. It is good to say thanks for the great witness of faith and belief offered to us by the many people who come and go to this church in the middle of their shopping. *Do I take time to stop and pray in the middle of my hurry? How do I share out my donations to the needy of the city and the people begging in the streets? How might they be feeling right now? Have I ever had the experience of begging? How did it feel?*

Back on Grafton St, retrace you steps as far as South Anne Street and walk to:

Station 5. St Anne's Church, Dawson St

The parish of St Anne's was founded in 1707 and the building of the church commenced around 1720. In this church religious and cultural activities take place at lunch time and in the evenings. The book shop beside the church is a great source of Christian publications. This is a chance to reflect on the reading in your life. *What cultural activities are part of your life? What poem or prose writing speaks to your soul? Have you a poem in your heart right now? Perhaps this is a chance to share your thoughts with God in poetry.*

Outside the church turn right and first right again to Molesworth Street. As you walk along, note the Grand Lodge, the headquarters of the Irish Constitution of Freemasons. It is the second oldest lodge in the world. On Kildare Street enter:

Station 6. The Early Christian Art Section of the National Museum

Try not to be distracted by the many beautiful artifacts to be seen here and go straight to the Early Christian Art section to the right of the main hall. A video presentation helps to draw you back to the early days of Christianity in Ireland. Let the beauty of these art pieces speak their story. The detailed art, design and crafts work that is evident in all the pieces is one of the finest of its time, long before the help of modern technology! *What church treasures are we passing on today? What artistic pieces do I treasure in my life and why?*

On Kildare street walk towards St Stephen's Green and turn left past the Shelbourne Hotel to Merrion Row. On the left is:

Station 7. The Huguenot Graveyard

An Act was passed in 1662 to 'Encourage Protestant Strangers to Settle in Ireland'. The French Huguenots arrived after the revocation of the Edict of Nantes in 1685. A congregation of French Huguenots were given the Lady Chapel in St Patrick's Cathedral. It is good to know that the city gave a welcome to the stranger. Today we have many refugees coming to Ireland fleeing from different forms of suffering and persecution. *What am I doing to help make these people welcome? What is going on in my mind and heart when I meet them on the street? Have I got to know any body who is a stranger to the city, in a personal way? When was I stranger in a foreign land? How did it feel? Jesus went into exile with his parents at a very young age, he knows what being an 'outsider' is like.*

Turn left onto Merrion Square and walk to:

Station 8. The National Art Gallery

An art gallery is worth a visit at any time. It is a place to meander and be with the images before you. Some will attract your attention, others just bore you. At times it is good not to look at the titles or the artists' names as these can often have undue influence on our responses. On this visit it is good to concentrate on one or two paintings; *The Taking of Christ* and *The Flight into Egypt*. Simply stay with the pictures and let them speak.

Perhaps place yourself inside one of the characters and ask what your thoughts and feelings might be if you were in that situation. Become aware of the message that is being conveyed to you by the artist. These are moments in the life of Jesus. Talk to Jesus about them and what it was like for him.

Leaving the Art Gallery, cross the road to:

Station 9. Archbishop Ryan Park, Merrion Square

Like St Stephen's Green, this is an oasis of greenery in a city of bricks and mortar. Let your senses feast on the life it offers as you walk through the gardens. At the far north-east corner there are two stone monuments: one is a remembrance of all the babies who have died in the Holles Street maternity hospital near-by; the second is an acknowledgement of the children who have suffered abuse in one form or another. Pray for these children and ask for a sensitivity to the deep pain and suffering they endured. *Who are the children that I meet who are most in need of care at this time? Hold them in your heart before God.*

When you return to Merrion Street, turn right and left on to Westland Row. You come to:

Station 10. The Church of St Andrew, Westland Row

St Andrew's was the first church to be built in the inner city on a main thoroughfare following Catholic Emancipation in 1829. Daniel O Connell was instrumental in the building of the church, the new home of the congregation that had worshiped in a small house in Townsend Street for over 80 years. One is immediately struck by the sense of space on entering the church. It has an open and expansive sanctuary which lends itself to ceremonies, many of which have taken place in the church. It was also the place of baptism for children born in Holles Street in the days when they were baptised shortly after birth. This might be a time to remember some church ceremony that stands out in your memory. *Who were the people involved and where are they now? Today it is good to remember all who have worshipped in this church, on great and small occasions.*

On Westland Row turn right and left and walk down Pearse Street to the front gate of:

Station 11. Trinity College. The Book of Kells

The college is famed for its great treasures including the *Book of Kells,* a 9th century illuminated manuscript. Originally a single volume, the 340 skin leaves were rebound in 1953 into four volumes. Pigments for the marvellous and intricate illustrations came from the Mediterranean and Central Asia. Notice the detail and the work in each letter. Give thanks for the talent and gifts that created this manuscript. Ponder the words being written. *What phrase or story in the gospels speaks most to you at this time and why? What in the gospels do I want to share at this time? What writing have I done lately?*

Pilgrimage End

Having spent some time with the *Book of Kells,* sitting in one of the many green spaces in the college or having a cup of coffee, it is good to celebrate and share a little of the pilgrimage experience with your companions. How did you experience some of the elements of pilgrimage? What place in the pilgrimage spoke to your faith? What have you remembered from all the people and things that you have seen and heard and why? What rituals did you feel called to pray? What grace do you feel you have received through this pilgrimage? What will you tell your friends when you return? How has the pilgrimage changed you? Perhaps in the group or on your own, you might share some of the prayers for a journey's end in the liturgy section.

Route 3: North Inner City

Key to the map:
1. Blessed Sacrament Chapel, Batchelor's Walk
2. Statues of Daniel O Connell & Fr Mathew, O Connell St
3. Pro-Cathedral, Marlborough St
4. Our Lady of Lourdes Church: Body of Matt Talbot, Sean Mc Dermott St
5. St Francis Xavier Church: Body of Fr John Sullivan, Gardiner St
6. Garden of Remembrance, Parnell Square
7. St Saviour's, Dominick St
8. St Mary's Abbey, Meeting House Lane
9. St Michan's Catholic Church, Halston St
10. St Mary of the Angels, Capuchin Church, Church St
11. St Michan's Church of Ireland, Church St

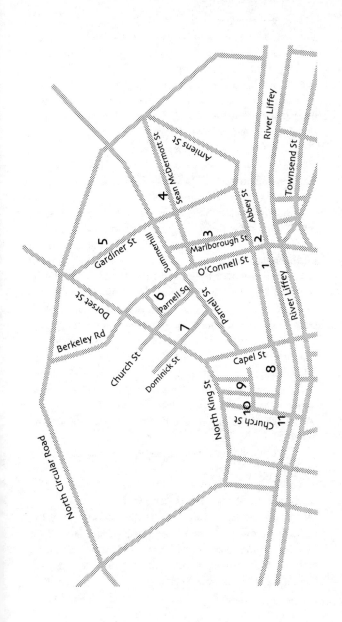

This pilgrimage begins at
Station 1. The Blessed Sacrament Chapel
The Blessed Sacrament chapel was dedicated and opened in 1995. It is a place of eucharistic adoration, celebration and reconciliation. It is an oasis in the heart of the city. This is a good time to put into words, the gift you want from this pilgrimage. *Who do I want to pray for or what is it that I want to be healed of as I visit these sacred places?*
On leaving the Blessed Sacrament chapel walk left towards:

Station 2. Statues of Daniel O Connell and Fr Mathew, O Connell St
O Connell Street is the main artery of the city and is constantly buzzing with life. It has a rich history and buildings that are part of the birth and life of the nation. At the southern end, as you enter the street, is a statue of Daniel O Connell, guarded by four angels. At the north end is a statue of Fr Mathew, the apostle of temperance. Both of these people have had great influence on the lives of the people all over the country and indeed abroad. As you give thanks for their lives, it is good to remember the people who have worked tirelessly for a peaceful solution to political struggles and conflicts. *How do I face conflict or support peaceful resolution to problems in my own life? What significance do these people have in today's world? How have I seen the influence of addiction in my own or in other peoples lives and what am I doing about it?*
From O Connell Street turn left and walk east along Cathedral Street to:

Station 3. St Mary's Pro-Cathedral
Daniel O Connell's words at the dedication of the Pro-Cathedral are as apt today as they were in 1825: 'If all classes of Irish people were united, if the demon of discord was cast out from among them, what a happy country, how blessed beyond example Ireland should be.'

This great church belongs to the people of Dublin, who

know it affectionately as the 'Pro'. Three stained glass windows showing Mary the Mother of God, St Kevin and St Laurence O'Toole, co-patrons of the archdiocese, light the back of the altar. Every day there is a constant stream of people dropping in to light a candle and say a prayer. It is a living church. It continues to be a heart for the city. *Watch the people as they come and go. Try to imagine their world as they reveal themselves through their faces, their dress or the time they spend as they come and go.*

When you leave the church turn left as far as Sean Mc Dermott Street. Turn right and walk to:

Station 4. Our Lady of Lourdes Church, Sean McDermott Street

On the left of the main aisle is the shrine of Matt Talbot 1856-1925. The casket which contains his body is in the centre. On the left are some pictures showing people and places in Matt Talbot's life and on the right the removal of the remains from Glasnevin Cemetery to Sean Mc Dermott Street church. Matt Talbot's triumph over addiction makes him a wonderful example and role model for people who struggle with addiction in their lives. Matt was committed to his work, no matter how humble, and devoted to a life of prayer and penance. *As you kneel, it is good to pray for healing and relief from all addictions, no matter how acceptable or unacceptable they may be. Pray that we might all be a support to each other through prayer and example.* On the right of the main aisle is a sacred space dedicated to justice and peace. On the back wall is the blanket showing the names of many young people who have died from addiction in the area. Remember these and their families and friends.

Back on Sean Mc Dermott St, turn right to Gardiner Street. Turn right again, passing Ozanam House of the St Vincent de Paul Society, and Mountjoy square on the right to:

Station 5. Church of St Francis Xavier, Gardiner St

The crucifixion scene providing the backdrop to the sanctuary and main altar in the church catches your eye as you enter. On the left side of the main aisle is the shrine to the Sacred Heart of Jesus, a devotion which has always been a central part of Ignatian Spirituality. Beside the shrine is a casket containing the remains of Fr John Sullivan, SJ, a man known for his great commitment and saintliness. On the opposite side of the church is the Lady Chapel where a constant stream of people come to pray at the shrine and light a candle.

The prayer of Ignatius: *Teach me to be generous, to give and not to count the cost. To toil and not to seek for rest. To labour and seek no reward, save that of knowing I do you will.*

Outside the church retrace your steps to Gardiner Place. Turn right and walk to Parnell Square, passing Belvedere College. As you walk notice the beautiful spire of Abbey Presbyterian Church. It is soaring to the sky and lifts our minds and hearts upwards. Cross the road to:

Station 6. The Garden of Remembrance

This is a garden dedicated to the lives of all who gave themselves for the cause of Irish freedom. The sculpture depicting an early mythological story shows the Children of Lir being changed into swans for 900 years. Freedom comes with new life from St Patrick and Christianity. Here we have many people to remember: those who die in war and through violence, those who fight for justice, political leaders, and those who make decisions in war. Often the people who suffer most are the refugees, the wounded, innocent victims and the families that have been bereaved. *In a particular way, pray for all these people who are walking the city today. May they find a little peace here in this garden.* From Parnell Square, walk around the garden turning right onto Parnell Square west as far as Dorset Street. Turn right and walk to Dominick Street to:

Station 7. The Church of St Saviour's

This is a quiet church, but the centre of life for the Order of Preachers in the city. Their medieval foundation was on the site now occupied by the Four Courts. It is one of the finest examples of Gothic revival in Ireland. The Blessed Sacrament Chapel is to the right with a tabernacle designed by Ray Carroll. For many people the shrine to St Martin De Pores on the left of the main altar is a place of refuge and strength as they come to him with their prayers and petitions.

Take time to remember all who have prayed in this church and the work done by the Dominican Fathers and Sisters in the city.

On Dominick St walk left to Parnell St. Turn right and walk to Capel Street, and turn right again to::

Station 8. St Mary's Abbey Chapter House, Meeting House Lane

Standing eight feet below the present street level, the Chapter House 1190 is the only section of the Cistercian Abbey in medieval Dublin to survive. The statue of Our Lady of Dublin in the Carmelite Church in Whitefriar Street was originally in St Mary's. These ruins serve as a reminder to us that all buildings and religious movements have their high and low moments in history. The church will rise and fall depending on its people, the culture of the time and factors beyond our control. God is above and beyond all our efforts to control and define the spiritual and its expression in our lives.

Stay with this sense of the passing of time and at what perhaps will be the ruins of our religious buildings in years to come.

Back on Capel Street, turn left into Brittan Street Little to:

Station 9 & 10. St Michan's Church, Halston St, St Mary of the Angels Capuchin Church, Church St

St Michan's is one of the oldest Catholic churches serving a Christian community in the inner city. It is tucked away off the beaten track, but in the heart of the markets area.

This is the nearest reminder we have today of what life might have been like in the city over the centuries. Take time to talk to the market people. Ponder on their work and the importance of it for our lives. *Do I appreciate the gift of food? How and when have I shared food with others recently?*

The Capuchin church is dedicated to St Mary of the Angels and has served not only the local community but people from the beyond the city through its sodalities and third order of St Francis. Religious orders have been very influential in the faith life of the people of Dublin. Perhaps this is a good time to say thanks for their generosity over the years. *How am I sharing my faith today and ensuring it is passed on to others?*

Station 11. St Michan's, Church Street

St Michan's occupies the site of an old Danish church of the eleventh century. Since approximately 1563 it has been with the Church of Ireland. The present church dates from 1680 with parts of it having been rebuilt at the beginning of this century. An effigy of the Danish bishop and confessor, St Michan, can be found in the south side of the chancel. A strong tradition has it that Handel played on this organ during his stay in Dublin at the time of the premiere of his oratorio, *The Messiah* in 1742. A panel in front of the organ consists of seventeen musical instruments, carved out of one piece of wood. In the vaults beneath the church, bodies have been mummified, due to the unique characteristic of the air in the basement. Some are said to be of the crusaders.

Regardless of who they are, they serve to remind us of the passing of time. A walk in the old cemetery at the back of the church also takes us back in time.

Pilgrimage end
This is a good place to end the pilgrimage and share some thoughts and reflections on the places visited and the people you met along the way. *How did you experience some of the elements of Pilgrimage? How did you experience a sense of community? Where did you feel a call to forgiveness? What rituals did you experience along the way?* It is good to end the pilgrimage with prayer together and the gift that this group has shared in the walk. (See section on Liturgy.)

OTHER HOLY PLACES IN DUBLIN DIOCESE

Glendalough is the central place of pilgrimage for the Archdiocese of Dublin. The diocese is rich in many other places blessed with a long Christian tradition both in the city of Dublin and throughout the counties of the diocese. The better known places have been mentioned in the pilgrimage routes in the city but the following is a list of the better known holy places beyond the city centre. The list is by no means exhaustive. There are many holy places that are known only to a local parish or community. These too could be explored as possible places of pilgrimage.

Other places of Pilgrimage in the City
Mercy Centre, Catherine MacAuley's Grave, Baggot St.
Christian Brothers Centre: Edmund Rice, O Connell's
    Schools, N. Richmond St.
Clonliffe College Chapel, Cardinal Cullen's Tomb,
    Clonliffe College Chapel.
All Hallows College, Grace Park Road.

Pilgrimage in the Outer City
Papal Cross, Phoenix Park.
St Bridget's Well, Castleknock.
St Patrick's Well, Finglas.
St Margaret's Well, (St Canice's Parish), Finglas.
Glasnevin Holy Faith Convent: Margaret Aylward's Grave
    Glasnevin.
Glasnevin Cemetery, Glasnevin.
Lady's Well, Mulhuddart.
St Donagh's Well, Kilbarrack.
Mount Jerome Cemetery, Harold's Cross.
Blessed Charles' Relics, Passionist Monastery, Mount
    Argus.

Rathfarnham Abbey, Burial of Frances Teresa Ball, Rathfarnham.

Religious Sister's of Charity Convent Cemetery, Body of Mary Aitkenhead, Donnybrook.

Deansgrange Cemetery, Deansgrange.

St Moling's Well, Tobar na gCluas, St Colmcille's Well, Monastic Ruins: Céile Dé, St Maelruin's Graveyard and Tree, Tallaght.

Mass Rock, Ballinascorney.

Bridget's Well, Round Tower, High Cross, Clondalkin.

St Kevin's Well, Kilnamanagh.

Co Dublin

St Begnet's Well and Churches, Dalkey.

St Nessan's Church, Ireland's Eye, Howth.

Round Tower, Lusk.

St MacCullin's Well, St Catherine's Well, Shrine of St Patrick's Staff, St Fintan's Well, Church and Graveyard, Sutton.

St Colmcille's Well, Swords.

Shrine of St Patrick's Staff, Ballyboughill.

St Doulagh's Church and Cross, Kinsealy.

Co Wicklow

St Kevin's Monastic City and Well, Glendalough.

Mass Rock, Hollywood.

Co Kildare

St Laurence O Toole's Birthplace.

Ruins of a Franciscan Friary, Kilkee, Castledermot.

High Cross, St Patrick's Well, Moone.

Round Tower, Taghadae, Lady Chapel Cemeteries, Laraghbryan.

Holy Wells, Maynooth.

St Patrick's College and Museum, Maynooth.

Pilgrimage Routes to include some of the above sacred places and introduce new ones to form stations along the way could be devised in local areas, e.g.:

Clondalkin Area

Station 1	Local Parish Church
Station 2	St. Cuthbert's Monastic Ruins, Kilmahudderick
Station 3	Camac River and Bridge
Station 4	Round Tower
Station 5	High Cross and Church of Ireland Church
Station 6	Village Catholic Church, Shrine of Our Lady
Station 7	St Bridget's Well
Station 8	Celebration – Local 'Gathering Place'

A similar Pilgrimage Route could be drawn up in Tallaght, Blanchardstown, Finglas, Dalkey, Lusk, Swords and any other local area or cluster of parishes in the diocese.

PART FIVE

PILGRIMAGE LITURGIES

_____ Section 18 _____

A: A GATHERING LITURGY
SETTING OUT ON A JOURNEY

A liturgy for pilgrims, as they gather together to begin the
pilgrimage, could be prayed at the home parish church, or
point of departure of the group. It could also be prayed at
the pilgrimage site, before the group begins the stations.

In the name of the Father,	*In ainm Athar,*
In the name of the Son,	*In ainm Mic,*
In the name of the Spirit,	*In ainm Spioraid,*
Three in One.	*Trí san Aon.*
May the Father protect me,	*Caomhnaíodh Athair mé,*
May the Son protect me,	*Caomhnaíodh Mac mé,*
May the Spirit protect me,	*Caomhnaíodh Spiorad mé,*
All-merciful King.	*Rí uilechaomh.*
May the Father sanctify me,	*Naomhaíodh Dia mé,*
May the Son sanctify me,	*Naomhaíodh Críost mé,*
May the Spirit sanctify me,	*Naomhaíodh Spiorad mé,*
All-holy Three.	*Trí uilenaomh.*

May the Three help my wishing,	*Cúnadh Trí mo dhúil,*
May the Three help my willing,	*Cúnadh Trí mo rún,*
May the Three help my walking,	*Cúnadh Trí mo shiúl,*
And my knees without weakening,	*Agus mo ghlúin gan chlaon.*

Christ Be Near At Either Hand

Christ be near at either hand
Christ behind, before me stand
Christ with me where e'er I go,
Christ around, above, below.

Christ be in my heart and mind,
Christ within my soul enshrined,
Christ control my wayward heart;
Christ abide and ne'er depart.

Christ my life and only way,
Christ my lantern night and day;
Christ be my unchanging friend,
Guide and shepherd to the end.

Scripture Reading: Isaiah 55:1-3, 6, 10-11

Everyone who thirsts, come to the waters;
and you that have no money, come, buy and eat!
Come, buy wine and milk
without money and without price.
Why do you spend your money for that which is not bread,
and your labour for that which does not satisfy?
Listen carefully to me, and eat what is good
and delight yourselves in rich food.
Incline your ear, and come to me;
listen, so that you may live.

Seek the Lord while he may be found,
call upon him while he is near;

For as the rain and the snow
come down from heaven,
and do not return there until
they have watered the earth,
making it bring forth and sprout,
giving seed to the sower and bread to the eater,
so shall my word be that goes out from my mouth;
it shall not return to me empty,

but it shall accomplish that which I purpose,
and succeed in the thing for which I sent it.
This is the word of the Lord.
Thanks be to God.

Reading

The actions of pilgrimage reveal some steps that we take as pilgrims on our journey. We become a reflection of the life of faith as a whole:

> *departure* reveals our decision as pilgrims to go forward to our destination and to be open to the spiritual wonder of our baptismal call;
>
> *walking* leads us in solidarity with our sisters and brothers in the necessary preparation for a meeting with God;
>
> *the visit* to the sacred places invites us to listen to the word of God, to listen to where God is in our lives and to sacramental celebration of the turning points of our lives;
>
> *the return,* in the end, reminds us of our own task in life, as witnesses of hope.

Quiet Reflection

Intercessions

The Lord's Prayer

Missioning of the Pilgrims

Holy Trinity, gathered here today, we place ourselves in
　　your care.
In the open air, surrounded by nature,
We are aware of the seasons as we walk.
We remember the holiness of this time and
The holy women and men of the past
　　that we are honouring.
Help us to see and hear the witness of their lives
　　in this holy place,
With a mind and heart that is open and generous.

Each person gathered has a pilgrim cross (and a pilgrim pack).
This is to remind us of the little we need for the journey.
We carry in our pilgrim bags,
A pilgrim scarf, some food and drink, a pilgrim cross.
A pilgrim staff helps us along the way.

Blessing of the Pilgrim and the Cross
In ainm an Athar a fuair bua,
Agus an Mhic a d'fhulaing an Pháis,
A Spiorad Naoimh, bí dár neartú,
Is a Mhaighdean ghlórmhar, bí inár dtriall.

(In the name of the Father who won victory,
In the name of the Son who suffered the passion,
O Holy Spirit, bring us strength,
O glorious Virgin, come to us.)

Bless each pilgrim on this journey.
Bless this cross as a sign of our pilgrimage.
May all who wear this cross,
    carry it with courage and confidence.
May we always reach out to our pilgrim companions and
Trust in God our saviour and friend.

Pilgrimage Prayer (All)
Life-giving God, we thank you.
You have always watched over our journeyings.
You have blessed us with signs of your presence.
We come to you now as we find ourselves
Needing to take up the staff of pilgrimage once more.
We are in need of energy and renewed hope.
We are in need of your grace
To unsettle and redirect our hearts.

Creating God,
May we go forward
Ever mindful of your truth,
Which leads and guides us.
We pray this through Jesus our brother. Amen.

Blessing

May God bless us and keep us.
May God's face shine on us and be gracious to us,
Be uncovered to us and bring us peace,
As we go forward with new faith, new hope and new love.

St Patrick's Breastplate

As the pilgrims set out on their journey, the music version, *The
Deer's Cry* from *The Pilgrim*, CD or Tape, by Shaun Davey could
be played, or the pilgrims could say it together..

I arise today, through God's strength to pilot me,
God's might to uphold me,
God's wisdom to guide me,
God's eye to look before me,
God's ear to hear me,
God's word to speak for me,
God's hand to guard me,
God's way to lie before me,
God's shield to protect me,
God's host to save me
From snares of devils, from temptations of vices,
From everyone who shall wish me ill,
Afar and anear, alone and in a multitude.

Christ in me, Christ beneath me, Christ above,
Christ on my right, Christ on my left,
Christ when I lie down, Christ when I sit down, Christ
when I arise,
Christ in the heart of everyone who thinks of me,
Christ in the mouth of everyone who speaks of me,
Christ in every eye that sees me,
Christ in every heart that hears me.
I arise today
Through a mighty strength, the invocation of the Trinity,
Through belief in the threeness,
Through confession of the oneness
Of the Creator of Creation.

B: PRAYER AND RITUALS
FOR STATION POINTS ALONG THE WAY

Depending on the pilgrimage, it may be helpful to give different groups or individuals responsibility for prayer at each station. The prayer and ritual for each station is unique to a particular pilgrimage. It is usual to give a theme to a station if it does not already have one by its nature or place. The following are some of the rituals and prayers that may be shared along the way and at station points. Portable amplification is an invaluable asset to gather the pilgrims at a station point.

1. Monastery or church ruins or present day church
2. High Cross
3. Holy Well
4. Statue
5. Graveyard
6. River Bridge
7. Stone Mound
8. Mountain and Hill
9. Prayers for Peace and Reconciliation

1. A Monastery or Church Ruin or present day Church

On arrival, circle the building or ruins and sense the character and spirit of the place. Try to imagine those who lived and worshipped in this sacred site many years or centuries before. If it is a place of worship today, remember the people of the area and the visitors. This may be a place to reflect on why one has come on pilgrimage, who we are and where we have come from. What monuments for our faith are we leaving behind for future generations?

Prayer
Holy Trinity, God,
from your chosen people,
you built an eternal church to your glory.
Increase the spiritual gifts you have given to your church,
so that your faithful people may continue to grow
into the new and eternal Jerusalem.

As the pilgrims enter these sacred places it is good to do so in silence. Then perhaps touch the stones, circle the inside of the building and, facing east – usually the end where the altar was placed – pray in thanksgiving for the gift of faith and the Eucharist. Churches are gathering places for the community. With what community do I share my faith?

Peter 2:4-9
So that you too may be living stones making a spiritual house.
Come to him, a living stone, though rejected by mortals yet chosen and precious in God's sight, and like living stones, let yourselves be built into a spiritual house, to be a holy priesthood, to offer spiritual sacrifices acceptable to God through Jesus Christ. For it stands in scripture: 'See, I am laying in Zion a stone, cornerstone chosen and precious; and whoever believes in him will not be put to shame.' To you then who believe, he is precious; but for those who do not believe, 'The stone that the builders rejected has become the very head of the corner,' and 'A stone that makes them stumble and a rock that makes them fall.' They stumble because they disobey the word, as they were destined to do. But you are a chosen race, a royal priesthood, a holy nation, God's own people, in order that you may proclaim the mighty acts of him who called you out of darkness into his marvellous light.
The Word of the Lord.

Prayer
God, you called your people to be your church.
As we gather together in your name,
may we love, honour, and follow you
to eternal life in the kingdom you promise.

As you leave this sacred place, usually by the west door you enter the world of nature around you. Beyond the church grounds you enter the sacred place of peoples home life, the city or the country. Listen to the sounds, smell the air and see what life is like for the local people who have come to this place over the years. Pray for a new consciousness of the interdependence of all of creation.

2. High Cross and Carved Stone

On approaching the cross or stone the pilgrim stands and bows to the sacredness of its memory. In some places it is tradition to circle the cross a number of times. This is always done *ciorcal deisial*, clockwise, right hand to the stone and in order to be at one with the motion of the universe. All of us experience the 'cross' in some form in our lives. For many it is the point of reconciliation and so we have a chance to pray for forgiveness for our sinfulness.

Matthew 5:23-24
Go and be reconciled with your brother, and then present your offering.
So when you are offering your gift at the altar, if you remember that your brother or sister has something against you, leave your gift there before the altar and go; first be reconciled to your brother or sister, and then come and offer your gift.
The Gospel of the Lord.

Having Confessed
Having confessed he feels
That he should go down on his knees and pray
For forgiveness for his pride, for having
Dared to view his soul from the outside.
Lie at the heart of the emotion, time
Has its own work to do. We must not anticipate
Or awaken for a moment. God cannot catch us
Unless we stay in the unconscious room
Of our hearts. We must be nothing,
Nothing that God may make us something.
We must not touch the immortal material
We must not daydream tomorrow's judgement –
God must be allowed to surprise us.
We have sinned, sinned like Lucifer
By this anticipation. Let us lie down again
Deep in anonymous humility and God
may find us worthy material for his hand.
Patrick Kavanagh

Local traditions have their own rituals for high crosses, e.g. in Glendalough local belief holds that a person who can stand with their back to St Kevin's cross, stretching their arms behind them until their fingers touch, will have their wish granted.

Before leaving the cross, the pilgrims join arms with another or place a hand on the cross or stone while praying for forgiveness. This can be a gesture of trust in God's presence and forgiveness.

3. A Holy Well
On the approach to the well, pilgrims collect three stones. These are placed beside the cross or statue after each circling of the well.

Song
Water of Life.
Jesus our Light.
Journey from death to new life.
David Haas

Praise and thanksgiving to you, O Holy Trinity.
Who made the heavens and the earth.
Who made fire, air and water.
We celebrate our creation and
The salvation won for us by the life, death and
Resurrection of Jesus.

Bless again ✠ this water, source of life and nourishment,
It gives fullness to all living things and
Refreshes and cleanses us.
Protect us from all danger, ill health and broken dreams.
May we always thirst for you, knowing that you
Alone can satisfy our quest for freedom and wholeness.
Give us living water,
Today and always and bring us to
Salvation and new life.

Scripture Reading: John 4:11-14
The woman said to him, 'Sir, you have no bucket, and the well is deep. Where do you get that living water? Are you greater than our ancestor Jacob, who gave us the well, and with his sons and his flocks drank from it?' Jesus said to her, 'Everyone who drinks of this water will be thirsty

again, but those who drink of the water that I will give will never be thirsty. The water that I will give will become in them a spring of water gushing up to eternal life.'
The Gospel of the Lord.

Ritual at the well
(As each one takes a drink from the well)
May God give me to drink from the well that never runs
    dry.
May God who made wine of the water at the wedding of
    Cana,
fill this water with strength and vigour.

Go dtuga Dia deoch duit as an tobar nach dtránn.
An té a rinne fíon den uisce ar bhainis Chána,
Go gcuire sé brí agus spreacadh san uisce seo.

(As the pilgrim walks around the well)
Health and praise to Jesus, who won new life for us.
Health to Mary, the Mother of Jesus
and Mother of Graces.

(Standing facing the tree beside the well or facing the sun.)
Health to all the saints of Ireland, living and dead,
Witnesses of the faith to us.

Let us pray:
God most high, God of hosts,
Lord of the world,
God invisible, God incorruptible,
God immortal, God all merciful,
God all perfect,
Fill us with your peace.

Intercessions

God of the earth, God of fire,
God of fresh waters, God of the great winds,
God of the shining stars, God who made the world,
God of the many tongues, God of the nations,
Make us messengers of your peace to all we meet.

Pilgrims circle the well again as they leave saying and singing:

Circle me O God, keep hope within, despair without.
Circle me O God, keep peace within, turmoil without.
Circle me O God, keep calm within, storms without.
Circle me O God, keep strength within, weakness without.
Circle me O God, keep wisdom within, foolishness without.

Song
We shall draw water joyfully, singing joyous music,
We shall draw water joyfully
   from the well springs of salvation.
Paul Inwood

4. Statue

A reading from the life of the saint, or prayers particularly associated with him or her, begins the station. Pilgrims often have a tradition of placing their hands on or kissing the feet of the statue as a mark of deep reverence for the memory of the saint. The values of the saint will often guide us in our prayers. Most of all they are reminders to us of the great gift we all share in the communion of saints, living and dead.

Ecclesiasticus 44:1-15
Their name lives on for all generations. (Reading from the Feast of All the Saints of Ireland).
Let us now sing the praises of famous people, our ancestors in their generations. The Lord apportioned to them great glory, his majesty from the beginning. There were those who ruled in their kingdoms, and made a name for themselves by their valour; those who gave counsel because they were intelligent; those who spoke in prophetic oracles; those who led the people by their counsels and by their knowledge of the people's lore; they were wise in their words of instruction; those who composed musical tunes, or put verses in writing; rich people endowed with resources, living peacefully in their homes – all these were honoured in their generations, and were the pride of their times. Some of them have left behind a name, so that others declare their praise. But of others there is no memory;

they have perished as though they have never existed; they have become as though they had never been born, they and their children after them. But these also were godly people, whose righteous deeds have not been forgotten; their wealth will remain with their descendants, and their inheritance with their children's children. Their descendants stand by the covenants; their children also, for their sake. Their offspring will continue forever, and their glory will never be blotted out. Their bodies are buried in peace, but their name lives on generation after generation. The assembly declares their wisdom, and the congregation proclaims their praise.

The Word of the Lord.

Prayer

You call us to announce your love and your vision;
to take a prophetic stance – for justice and for peace,
For the poor, the powerless and the lowly ones.
May we proclaim the sacredness of each person.
May we be Good News
As we minister and are ministered to.
Lord, may our pilgrimage together
Be an opportunity to give thanks,
To redefine our vision,
To search, and to be shaped and reshaped
Through reflection, interaction, challenge and your forming love.
May we find among us
The light of tomorrow's dreaming.

5. Graveyard

The ritual at a cemetery requires great reverence as we walk about the grounds. Usually it is best to stand beside a particular grave and so from this point to reach out to all who have died. In particular, it is important to remember those who have died alone, as refugees, as wandering souls who at last have found their peace with God.

Intercessions

As we gather with our ancestors who have kept the faith alive and passed it on to us, it is good to remember the words of Jesus: 'I am the resurrection and the life. Those who believe in me, even though they die, will live.' *(Jn 11:25)*.

Response: All our hope is in your promise.

In death, life is changed, not taken away;
make us open in this life to your call to growth. R.

Time passes swiftly; we do not know the day of death;
Help us to cherish the lifetime given to us and make
each moment a preparation for our last. R.

You promised eternal life to all who follow your way;
raise up all who have died, particularly those we have loved
and those who have loved us;
grant that we may share eternal glory with them. R.

Prayer

O God, our birth is the fruit of your live; our redemption, the fruit of your mercy. Help us to remember your generosity and make our lives a worthy revelation of your care. Let the hour of death be a longed-for reunion with you, our Creator, Saviour, and Sanctifier. Amen.

6. River/Bridge

For many the best ritual is simply to stand or sit on the bank of a river or stream and listen to the flowing water. Let the waters speak. Listen to the sound of the water, the birds, the distant voices. It is good to throw a stone or a leaf in the water and let it flow away with one's prayers and intentions. Some people like to step into the water. The washing of one's own feet or those of another is a sign of service and reverence.

Genesis 28:11-18
House of God and the Gate of Heaven

He came to a certain place and stayed there for the night, because the sun had set. Taking one of the stones of the place, he put it under his head and lay down in that place.

And he dreamed that there was a ladder set up on the earth, the top of it reaching to heaven; and the angels of God were ascending and descending on it. And the Lord stood beside him and said, 'I am the Lord, the God of Abraham your father and the God of Isaac; the land on which you lie I will give to you and to your offspring; and your offspring shall be like the dust of the earth, and shall spread abroad to the west and to the east and to the north and to the south; and all the families of the earth shall be blessed in you and in your offspring. Know that I am with you and will keep you wherever you go and bring you back to this land; for I will not leave you until I have done what I have promised you.' Then Jacob woke from his sleep and said, 'Surely the Lord is in this place – and I did not know it!' And he was afraid, and said, 'How awesome is this place! This is none other than the house of God, and this is the gate of heaven.' So Jacob rose early in the morning, and he took the stone that he had put under his head and set it up for a pillar and poured oil on the top of it.
The Word of the Lord.

Crossing a bridge is in itself a ritual act. It is a passing through time and space to a new and unknown future, leaving the past with its failures and imperfections behind us.

7. Stone Mound
It is common in some pilgrimages to bring a stone and leave it at a certain station along the way or at the destination. There may also be a point at which the pilgrim collects a stone and takes it home as a mark of the new self. The pilgrim may also take a rounded stone, bless himself/herself with it, pass it to the back of the body and then to the front while invoking the Blessed Trinity. This ritual is carried out three times. Stones serve as a reminder in the coming year of the trials and tribulations of one's own pilgrimage and those of others along the way.

Prayer to the Trinity

The Three that are oldest, the Three that are youngest,
The Three that are strongest in the heaven of glory
 – the Father, the Son and Holy Spirit –
May they be saving and guarding us today and tonight, and
To a year from today and tonight.

Proof

I would like all things to be free of me,
Never to murder the days with presupposition,
Never to feel they suffer the imposition
Of having to be this or that. How easy
It is to maim the moment
With expectation, to force it to define
Itself. Beyond all that I am, the sun
Scatters its light as though by accident ...
Brendan Kennelly

8. Mountains and Hills

At some stage of the pilgrimage, preferably on a rise of ground,
on top of a hill, or on top of a building, look out over the world
around – a world of goodness and beauty, a world of rottenness
and evil. With all its tensions, stresses, temptations, it is our
world, it is God's world, both sinful and graced, a world in need
of continuing redemption.

Prayer for World Praise

God of the infinite spaces – Glory and praise to you.
God of sun, moon and stars – Glory and praise to you.
God of earth, sea and sky – Glory and praise to you.
God of grass and tree and flower – Glory and praise to you.
God of bird and beast and fish – Glory and praise to you.
God of sunshine, wind and rain – Glory and praise to you.
Father and lover of humanity – Glory and praise to you.

Intercession

We cry to you on behalf of the world
– God of mercy, hear our prayer.
That we may love and care for the earth, sea and air
– God of mercy, hear our prayer.
That we may love and care for all your creatures –
 God of mercy, hear our prayer.
That we may love and care for all your people
– God of mercy, hear our prayer.
For those whose humanity is destroyed by hunger
– God of mercy, hear our prayer.
For those whose humanity is destroyed by the abuse of power
– God of mercy, hear our prayer.
For those whose humanity is destroyed by the sins of others
– God of mercy, hear our prayer.
For all who are lost and lonely
– God of mercy, hear our prayer.
For all who are sick and dying
– God of mercy, hear our prayer.
For all whose hearts are broken
– God of mercy, hear our prayer.
For all who have lost the faith
– God of mercy, hear our prayer.
For all who do not know you
– God of mercy, hear our prayer.
For all who are prisoners of addiction
– God of mercy, hear our prayer.
For all who seek you sincerely
– God of mercy, hear our prayer.
For all who seek you in the wrong places
– God of mercy, hear our prayer.
For all who are lost in their own sins
– God of mercy, hear our prayer.
For all who struggle to make peace
– God of mercy, hear our prayer.
For all who struggle to do good
– God of mercy, hear our prayer.

For all who struggle to save others
– God of mercy, hear our prayer.
For all who have power and influence
– God of mercy, hear our prayer.
For all who are powerless and oppressed
– God of mercy, hear our prayer.
For your church in service of the world
– God of mercy, hear our prayer.
For all who are especially dear to our heart
– God of mercy, hear our prayer.
A Pilgrim in Celtic Scotland, J. J. Ó Ríordáin.

10. Prayers for Peace and Reconciliation

1. O God we thank you for the message of peace that Christmas brings to our distracted world. Give peace among the nations; peace in our land; peace in our homes; and peace in our hearts, as we remember the birth at Bethlehem of the Prince of peace, Jesus Christ our Lord, Amen.   From *Worship Now*

2. Sweet Child of Bethlehem, grant that we may share with all our hearts in the profound mystery of Christmas. Pour into our hearts the peace which we sometimes seek so desperately, and which you alone can give us. Help us to know one another better and to live as brothers, sisters, children of the same Father. Awaken in our hearts love and gratitude for your infinite goodness; join us together in your love; and give us all your heavenly peace.
Pope John XXIII (slightly altered)

3. Lord our God, grant us grace to desire you with our whole heart; that so desiring, we may seek and find you; and so finding, may love you; and so loving, may hate those sins from which you have delivered us; through Jesus Christ our Lord, Amen.   *Saint Anselm*

4. Have mercy, Lord, on our distracted and suffering world, on nations perplexed and divided. Give to us and to all people a new spirit of repentance and amendment; direct the counsels of all who are working for the removal of the causes of strife and for the promotion of goodwill, and hasten the coming of your kingdom of peace and love; through Jesus Christ our Lord, Amen.

Archbishop Charles d'Arcy

5. Loving Father, you have made us in your own likeness, and you love all whom you have made. Suffer not the world to separate itself from you by building barriers of race and colour. As your Son our Saviour was born of a Hebrew mother, yet rejoiced in the faith of a Syrian woman and a Roman soldier, welcomed the Greeks who sought him and suffered an African to carry his cross, so teach us rightly to regard the members of all races as fellow-heirs of your kingdom; through the same Jesus Christ our Lord, Amen.

Olive Warner

6. God of love, good beyond all that is good;
God of peace, in whom is calmness and concord;
Make up the dissensions that divide us one from another,
and bring us to that unity to which we are called
by your Son Jesus Christ our Lord, Amen.

From the Liturgy of St Dionysius

7. God eternal, in whom we live and move and have our being, awaken us to your presence that we may walk in your world as your children. Grant us reverence for your creation, that we may treat our brothers and sisters with courtesy, and all things living with gentleness, through Jesus Christ our Lord. Amen.

New Every Morning

8. For all the possibilities ahead in this new century make us thankful, O Lord. Give us wisdom, courage and discernment in the face of so much chaos, despair and fear. Help us to see how we can contribute towards peace, faith and love. and give us the will to translate our desires into actions. We ask this through Jesus Christ our Lord. Amen.

Brother John Charles SSF (adapted)

C: THE JOURNEY'S END

Prayers for the ending of a pilgrimage
My thanks to you, Father,
for the pilgrim journey I have undertaken.
My thanks for the strength and heart
to walk in your presence.

My thanks for your supporting love
along the way.
My thanks for rest and peace
now at the end of it all.

Here in your house
may I taste the peace of heaven,
may I taste the joy of being cleansed and forgiven,
may I taste the fullness of your love.

From this day forth
let all my journeys
echo with the meaning of this journey.
Wherever I go
let me bring with me an awareness of your presence
and the joy of your kingdom,
where you live with your Son and Holy Spirit,
one God forever and ever. Amen.
A Pilgrim in Celtic Scotland, J. J. Ó Ríordáin.

To Live With The Spirit

To live with the Spirit of God is to be a listener.
It is to keep the vigil of mystery,
earthless and still.
One leans to catch the stirring of the Spirit,
strange as the wind's will.

The soul that walks where the wind of the Spirit blows
turns life a wandering weather-vane toward love.
It may lament like Job or Jeremiah,
echo the wounded heart, the mateless dove.
It may rejoice in spaciousness of meadow
that emulates the freedom of the sky.
Always it walks in waylessness, unknowing;
it has cast down forever from its hand
the compass of the whither and the why.
To live with the Spirit of God is to be a lover.
It is becoming love, and like to him
toward whom we strain with metaphors of creatures;
fire-sweep and water-rush and with wind's whim.
The soul is all activity, all silence;
and though it surges God-ward to its goal,
it holds, as moving earth holds sleeping noonday,
The peace that is the listening of the soul.

Jessica Powers, Selected Poetry

God be in me

God be in my head,
And in my understanding;
God be in mine eyes,
And in my looking;
God be in my mouth,
And in my speaking;
God be in my heart,
And in my thinking;
God be at my end and at my departing.

Anonymous

Prayer for Ireland

God, we entrust to you today our hearts, our consciences, and our works, that they may be in keeping with the faith we profess. We entrust to you the community of the Irish people and the community of the People of God living in this land.

We entrust to you the mothers and fathers, the youth, the children. We entrust to you the bishops of Ireland, the clergy, the religious men and women, the contemplative monks and sisters, the seminarians, the novices. We entrust to you the teachers, the musicians, the catechists, the students, the writers, the poets, the actors, the artists, the workers and their leaders, the employers and managers, the professional people, the farmers, those engaged in political and public life, those who form public opinion. We entrust to you the married and those preparing for marriage, those called to serve you and others in single life, the sick, the aged, the mentally ill, the handicapped and all who nurse and care for them. We entrust to you the prisoners and all who feel rejected, the exiled, the homesick and the lonely.

We entrust to you God, the care of the land of Ireland, where you are so much loved. Help this land to stay true to you and your Son always. May prosperity never cause Irish women and men to forget God or abandon their faith. Keep them faithful in prosperity to the faith they would not surrender in poverty and persecution. Save them from greed, from envy, from seeking selfish or sectional interest. Help them to work together with a sense of Christian purpose and a common Christian goal, to build a just and peaceful and loving society where the poor are never neglected and the rights of all, especially the weak, are respected. Keep Ireland true to her spiritual tradition and her Christian heritage. Help her to respond to her historic mission of bringing the light of Christ to the nations, and so making the glory of God be the honour of Ireland.

Pope John Paul II, Ireland 1979.

LITURGY FOR YOUNG PEOPLE

Introduction

Lord, as we begin our pilgrimage, our journey in your name, lead us and guide us as we experience your presence in the knowledge that many people have walked this way before us. Help us to search for you and discover meaning in all that we do. As Jeremiah said, all those years ago:

'Stand at the crossroads and look,
ask for the ancient paths:
which was the good way? Take it
and you will find rest for yourselves.' Jer 6:16

Show us, Lord, the good way.
Give us rest in this busy world.
Help us to experience your way.
We make this our prayer in Jesus' name.
Amen.

Scripture: Psalm 25:4-10

Make me to know your ways, O Lord,
teach me your paths.
Lead me in your truth, and teach me,
for you are the God of my salvation;
for you I wait all day long.

Be mindful of your mercy,
O Lord, and of your steadfast love,
for they have been from of old.
Do not remember the sins of my youth
or my transgressions;
according to your steadfast love remember me,
for your goodness' sake, O Lord!

Good and upright is the Lord;
Therefore he instructs sinners in the way.

He leads the humble in what is right,
and teaches the humble his way.
All the paths of the Lord are
steadfast love and faithfulness,
for those who keep his covenant and his decrees.

An alternative scripture passage is Luke 24:13-36, The Road to Emmaus.

Quiet Time of Reflection

Mountain Prayer
I enjoyed the day in the mountains, Lord.
Seemed we were in the middle of your creation,
Surrounded by your peace and refreshment.

The air was fresh,
Sounds were clear as a bell,
It was like being at the beginning of something.
Even though these mountains
Have been here for centuries,
It seemed as if they were all just new that day.

Is that what you are like, Lord,
Always new, never ageing?
And we're like that too,
Even though we look the same.
We're new, strong, part of you.

Thanks, Lord, for creation:
For the strength of the mountains,
The pathways leading to the top,
The streams, the trees, the flowers, the animals we saw a
deer in the distance;
Thanks for the beauty and freshness and creation,
The beauty unites us in a good feeling together.

The mountains are strong like you, Lord.
And you are always making them,
It's not that you made them years ago
And now sit somewhere just watching them.

Your life keeps them strong and lovely.
You're always growing new trees,
Putting down deeper roots,
Giving fresh water to streams;
That's the way you make everything,
And you are all the time making us.

Help me, Lord, to know that you are always involved in my
growing up,
Your love grows me, makes me bigger, stronger, more alive,
And your love is the sure pathway of my life.
Please, Lord, let me be thankful for all you make,
And that you're making the best of me all the time,
Day by day, a loving glance each moment.

For this making of me, thank you, Lord.

Donal Neary, SJ,
Lighting the Shadows: Prayers and Reflections for Young People

Prayer of St Francis of Assisi
Make me a channel of your peace;
Where there is hatred, let me bring your love;
Where there is injury, your pardon, Lord,
And where there's doubt, true faith in you.

O Master grant that I may never seek
So much to be consoled as to console;
To be understood as to understand;
To be loved as to love with all my soul.

Make me a channel of your peace;
It is in pardoning that we are pardoned;
In giving to each one that we receive;
And in dying that we're born to eternal life.

Intercessions

Our Father

Conclusion
Young Person's Jubilee Prayer

God of my life,
Help me to appreciate
The special way
That you have gifted me,
So that I will be fully alive
And so that many others
Will be the better
For having met me or known me.

Help me to be free, loving and generous.
Give me a listening heart,
So that I will discover the things
That are really worth living for.
When I'm down and life is tough,
Don't let me lose heart,
And show me that you are always
There by my side.
Amen.

A: SCRIPTURE READINGS FOR PILGRIMAGE

Exodus 3:1-6
The presence of God in the desert and the call of Moses.
Moses was keeping the flock of his father-in-law Jethro, the priest of Midian; he led his flock beyond the wilderness, and came to Horeb, the mountain of God. There the angel of the Lord appeared to him in a flame of fire out of a bush; he looked, and the bush was blazing, yet it was not consumed. Then Moses said, 'I must turn aside and look at this great sight, and see why the bush is not burned up.' When the Lord saw that he had turned aside to see, God called to him out of the bush, 'Moses, Moses!' And he said, 'Here I am.' Then he said, 'Come no closer! Remove the sandals from your feet, for the place on which you are standing is holy ground.' He said further, 'I am the God of your father, the God of Abraham, the God of Isaac, and the God of Jacob.' And Moses hid his face, for he was afraid to look at God.

Isaiah 2:2-5
Even those who were once pagan nations go to Jerusalem: the word of God has changed the direction of their lives.
In days to come
the mountain of the Lord's house
shall be established as the highest of the mountains,
and shall be raised above the hills;
all the nations shall stream to it.
Many peoples shall come and say,
'Come, let us go up to the mountain of the Lord,
to the house of the God of Jacob;
that he may teach us his ways
and that we may walk in his paths.'
For out of Zion shall go forth instruction,

and the word of the Lord from Jerusalem.
He shall judge between the nations,
and shall arbitrate for many peoples;
they shall beat their swords into ploughshares,
and their spears into pruning hooks;
nation shall not lift up sword against nation, neither shall
they learn war no more.

O house of Jacob, come, let us walk
In the light of the Lord!

Psalm 122
The joy of going to God's house
I was glad when they said to me,
'Let us go to the house of the Lord!'
Our feet are standing
within your gates, O Jerusalem.

Jerusalem – built as a city
that is bound firmly together.
To it the tribes go up,
the tribes of the Lord,
as was decreed for Israel,
to give thanks for the name of the Lord.
For there the thrones for judgement were set up,
the thrones of the house of David.

Pray for the peace of Jerusalem:
'May they prosper who love you.
Peace be within your walls,
and security within your towers.'

For the sake of my relatives and friends
I will say, 'Peace be within you.'
For the sake of the house of the Lord our God,
I will seek your good.

Psalm 63

For you my soul is thirsting, O Lord, my God

O God you are my God, I seek you, my soul thirsts for you;
my flesh faints for you, as in a dry and weary land
where there is no water.
So I have looked upon you in the sanctuary,
beholding your power and glory.
Because your steadfast love is better than life,
my lips will praise you.
So I will bless you as long as I live;
I will lift up my hands and call on your name.

My soul is satisfied as with a rich feast,
and my mouth praises you with joyful lips
when I think of you on my bed,
and meditate on you in the watches of the night;
for you have been my help,
and in the shadow of your wings I sing for joy.
My soul clings to you; your right hand upholds me.

But those who seek to destroy my life
shall go down into the depths of the earth;
they shall be given over to the power of the sword,
they shall be prey for jackals.
But the king shall rejoice in God;
all who swear by him shall exult,
for the mouths of liars shall be stopped.

Hebrews 11:8-10, 13-16

By faith Abraham obeyed when he was called to set out for
a place that he was to receive as an inheritance; and he set
out not knowing where was going. By faith he stayed for a
time in the land he had been promised, as in a foreign land,
living in tents, as did Isaac and Jacob, who were heirs with
him of the same promise. For he looked forward to the city
that has foundations, whose architect and builder is God.

All of these died in faith without having received the
promises, but from a distance they saw and greeted them.

They confessed that they were strangers and foreigners on the earth. For people who speak in this way make it clear that they are seeking a homeland. If they had been thinking of the land that they had left behind, they would have had opportunity to return. But as it is, they desire a better country, that is a heavenly one. Therefore God is not ashamed to be called their God; indeed, he has prepared a city for them.

Matthew 2:13-15, 19-23

Now after they had left, an angel of the Lord appeared to Joseph in a dream and said, 'Get up, take the child and his mother, and flee to Egypt, and remain there until I tell you; for Herod is about to search for the child, to destroy him.' Then Joseph got up, took the child and his mother by night and went to Egypt, and remained there until the death of Herod. This was to fulfil what had been spoken by the Lord through his prophet, 'Out of Egypt I have called my son.'

When Herod died, an angel of the Lord suddenly appeared in a dream to Joseph in Egypt and said, 'Get up, take the child and his mother, and go to the land of Israel, for those who were seeking the child's life are dead'. Then Joseph got up, took the child and his mother, and went to the land of Israel. But when he heard that Archelaus was ruling over Judea in place of his father Herod, he was afraid to go there. And after being warned in a dream, he went away to the district of Galilee. There he made his home in a town called Nazareth, so that what had been spoken through the prophets might be fulfilled, 'He will be called a Nazarean'.

Additional Biblical Readings
on the theme of Pilgrimage

Gen 12:1-7 *Leaving home and going into the unknown.*

Gen 35:1-7 *Coming into God's presence is a call to let God be first in our lives.*

Exod 3:1-6 *Moses experiences God as fire that purifies, that heals his past.*

Exod 15:1-8 *The goal of Israel's journey is arrival in God's holy place.*

Exod 19:16-20; 24:12-18 *Moses' friendship with God is sealed with a covenant.*

1 Sam 1:1-3 *A pilgrimage to God's presence in order to honour God there.*

1 Kgs. 8:1-13 *The ark, sign of God's presence, is brought to Jerusalem.*

Is 2:2-5 *Even those who once were pagan nations go to Jerusalem: the word of God has changed the direction of their lives.*

Is 55:1-11 *God invites his people to come to him for he has great gifts to give.*

Is 61:1-4 *The Spirit of the Lord God is upon me.*

Jer 31:6-12 *God gathers his people to Jerusalem to rejoice over his goodness.*

Ps 42 (41) *Thirsting for God's presence, for his help.*

Ps 46 (45) *God is our refuge and our strength.*

Ps 63 (62) *Longing for God who is our help.*

Ps 84 (83) *Desire to be in the house of the Lord and to receive his favour.*

Ps 95 (94) *God is our God. We come to listen to him.*

Ps 100 (99) *Coming into God's presence with joy.*

Ps 118 (117) *A processional hymn in praise of God whose love is steadfast.*

Pss 120-125, esp. 122 and 125 *The joy of going to God's house.*

Acts 13: 1-4 *We are sent by the Spirit on pilgrimage.*

2 Cor 5:6-8 *On our pilgrimage we walk by faith and have good courage.*
Heb 9:11-14 *The arrival point of our final pilgrimage is heaven.*
Heb 11:1-40 *Our pilgrimage journey is made in faith.*
Heb 12:18-24 *Pilgrimage is a journey towards the heavenly Jerusalem.*
Rev 21:1-8 *In the new Jerusalem there will be no more tears, no death.*

Mt 21:1-11; Mk 11:1-11; Lk 19:28-35 *Jesus' journey brings him to the temple, the sacred place where God is specially available to his people.*
Lk 9:51-56 *Jesus set out on the journey that will bring him into his Father's presence.*
Lk 24:13-35 *Jesus is our companion on our pilgrimage journey.*
Jn 2:13-22 *Jesus goes on pilgrimage to Jerusalem for the feast of Passover.*
Jn 4:20-23 *God wants to be worshipped in spirit and in truth.*
Jn 12:12-19 *Jesus is welcomed into the holy city of Jerusalem.*
Jn 12:12-19 *Jesus brings peace and forgiveness of sin.*

B: HYMNS FOR PILGRIMAGE

The following is a selection of liturgical music suitable for use at different parts of a pilgrimage. Many of the hymns are taken from *Seinn Alleluia 2000*, a Jubilee collection of music prepared by the Advisory Committee on Church Music. The list is not exhaustive and every parish or group may have their own favourites to add, e.g. hymns to a saint associated with the local area.

Ag Críost an Síol
Ag Críost an síol, ag Críost an fómhar,
In iothalainn Dé go dtugtar sinn,
Ag Críost an mhuir, ag Críost an t-iasc,
I líonta Dé go gcastar sinn,
Ó fhás go haois, is ó aois go bás,
Do dhá láimh, a Chríost, anall tharainn,
Ó bhás go críoch, ní críoch ach athfhás,
I bParthas na nGrást go rabhaimid.

Traditional

How Lovely on the Mountains are the feet of him
How lovely on the mountains are the feet of one who
brings good news, good news,
Announcing peace, proclaiming news of happiness;
Our God reigns, our God reigns, – our God reigns,
Our God reigns, our God reigns, – our God reigns,

Leonard E. Smith Jr.

(See copyright acknowledgements on page 171)

Be Not Afraid

Refrain:
Be not afraid: I go before you always:
Come, follow me, and I will give you rest.

You shall cross the barren desert,
But you shall not die of thirst.
You shall wander far in safety,
Though you do not know the way.
You shall speak your words to foreign lands
And they will understand.
You shall see the face of God and live.

If you pass through raging waters
In the sea, you shall not drown.
If you walk among the burning flames,
You shall not be harmed.
If you stand before the power of hell
and death is at your side,
Know that I am with you through it all.

Blessed are your poor,
For the kingdom shall be theirs.
Blest are you that weep and mourn.
For one day you shall laugh.
And if wicked tongues insult and hate you
all because of me. Blessed, blessed are you!

Bob Dufford SJ

Taize Chants

Eat this bread, drink this cup,
come to him and never be hungry.
Eat this bread, drink this cup
trust in him and you will not thirst.

Jesus, remember me when you come
into your Kingdom.
Jesus, remember me when you come
into your Kingdom.

O Lord hear my pray'r,
O Lord hear my pray'r:
When I call answer me.
O Lord hear my pray'r,
O Lord hear my pray'r:
Come and listen to me.

Ubi caritas et amor,
Ubi caritas
Deus ibi est.

Music: Jacques Berthier (1923-1994)

The Light of Christ
Refrain:
The light of Christ has come into the world;
The light of Christ has come into the world.

All people must be born again
to see the Kingdom of God.
The water and the Spirit bring new life
in God's love. R.

God gave up his only Son
out of love for the world,
so that all people who believe in him
will live for ever. R.

The light of God has come to us
so that we might have salvation;
from the darkness of our sins we walk
into glory with Christ Jesus. R.

Donald Fishel

Deus Meus Adiuva Me

Deus meus adiuva me,
Tabhair dom do shearc, a Mhic dhil Dé,
Tabhair dom do shearc, a Mhic dhil Dé,
Deus meus adiuva me

Domine, da quod peto a te,
Tabhair dom go dian, a ghrian ghlan ghlé,
Tobhair dom go dian, a ghrian ghlan ghlé,
Domine, da quod peto a te.

Tuum amorem sicut vis,
Tabhair dom go tréan a déarfad arís,
Tabhair dom go tréan a déarfad arís,
Tuum amorem sicut vis.

Domine, Domine, exaudi me,
M'anam bheith lán ded' ghrá, a Dhé,
M'anam bheith lán ded' ghrá, a Dhé,
Domine, Domine, exaudi me

Maol Íosa Ó Brolcháin

My God, assist me,
Give me your love O Christ, I pray,
Give me your love O Christ, I pray,
My God, assist me.

Lord, grant what I ask of you,
O pure bright sun, give, give, today,
O pure bright sun, give, give, today,
Lord, grant what I ask of you.

Your love as you will,
Give to me swiftly, strongly, this,
Give to me swiftly, strongly, this,
Your love as you will.

Lord, Lord, hearken to me,
Fill my soul, Lord, with your love's ray,
Fill my soul, Lord, with your love's ray,
Lord, Lord, hearken to me.

A Mhuire na nGrás

A Mhuire na ngrás,
A Mháthair Mhic Dé,
Go gcuire tú
Ar mo leas mé.

Go sábhála tú mé
Ar muir is ar tír.
Go sábhála tú mé
Ar lic na bpian.

Garda na n-aingeal
Os mo chionn;
Dia romham
Is Dia liom.

O Mary of Graces

O Mary of graces and mother of Christ,
May you direct me and guide me aright,
O may you protect me from Satan's control,
And may you protect me in body and soul.

O may you protect me by land and by sea,
And may you protect me from sorrows to be,
A strong guard of angles above me provide,
May God be before me and God at my side.

J. Rafferty

Additional Hymns for Pilgrimage

Céad Míle Fáilte Romhat, A Íosa
Be Thou My Vision
Hail Glorious St Patrick
Dóchas Linn Naomh Pádraig
Christ Be Beside Me
Canaigí Amhrán Nua don Tiarna
Be Still and Know that I am God
Seek Ye First the Kingdom of God
Amazing Grace
A Channel of Your Peace
I Am the Bread of Life
The Lord's My Shepherd
All the Ends of the Earth
Stay with us Lord
May Your Love Be Upon Us O Lord
Let all the Peoples Praise You
Hail Mary Full of Grace
Salve Regina
How Great Thou Art
Shine, Jesus, Shine
Pilgrim Alleluia
Lord, You are My Shepherd
The Lord's Prayer
Jesus Remember Me
Hail Queen of Heaven
Gloria
As I Kneel Before You
Mo Ghrá Thú
Sé an Tiarna m'Aoire
On Eagles' Wings

Seasons
In quick or in slow succession, frost
into fire, fire into frost,
the seasons of the year return
and leave us numb with cold
or warm us, like the seasons of the heart.

But that last season you endured
- your heart's dark winter -
was so bleak and cold that still
to this day, to this hour,
the frost remains in your blood.

But now is the moment of change,
now the apocalypse.
Today, swept by the winds of another
season, the blossoms
of fruit trees are ablaze with colour.

Surely it is the end of spring,
the promised summer?
So say 'yes' and 'yes' again
to this moment
while it turns, for soon it will be gone.

And soon the trees of spring
will become the trees of memory,
and will be shaken by the powerful winds
of memory, cowering
like blown candles and blazing askew.

Paul Murray

The Primrose

Upon a bank I sat, a child made seer
Of one small primrose flowering in my mind.
Better than wealth it is, said I, to find
One small page of Truth's manuscript made clear.
The light was very beautiful and kind,
And where the Holy Ghost in flame had signed
I read it through the lenses of a tear.
And then my sight grew dim, I could not see
The primrose that had lighted me to heaven,
And there was but the shadow of a tree
Ghostly among the stars. The years that pass
Like tired soldiers nevermore have given
Moments to see wonders in the grass.

Patrick Kavanagh

The One

Green, blue, yellow and red –
God is down in the swamps and marshes
Sensational as April and almost incredible the flowering of
    our catharsis.
A humble scene in a backward place
Where no one important ever looked
The raving flowers looked up in the face
Of the One and the Endless, the Mind that has baulked
The profoundest of mortals. A primrose, a violet,
A violent wild iris – but mostly anonymous performers
Yet an important occasion as the Muse at her toilet
Prepared to inform the local farmers
That beautiful, beautiful, beautiful God
Was breathing his love by a cut-away bog.

Patrick Kavanagh

The Bright Field

I have seen the sun break through
to illuminate a small field
for a while, and gone my way
and forgotten it. But that was the pearl
of great price, the one field that had
the treasure in it. I realise now
that I must give all that I have
to possess it. Life is not hurrying

on to a receding future, nor hankering after
an imagined past. It is the turning
aside like Moses to the miracle
of the lit bush, to a brightness
that seemed as transitory as your youth
once, but is the eternity that awaits you.

R. S. Thomas

The Kingdom

It's a long way off but inside it
There are quite different things going on:
Festivals at which the poor man
Is king and the consumptive is
Healed; mirrors in which the blind look
At themselves and love looks at them
Back; and industry is for mending
The bent bones and the minds fractured
By life. It's a long way off, but to get
There takes no time and admission
Is free, if you will purge yourself
Of desire, and present yourself with
Your need only and the simple offering
Of your faith, green as a leaf.

R. S. Thomas

Somewhere

Something to bring back to show
you have been there: a lock of God's
hair, stolen from him while he was
asleep; a photograph of the garden
of the spirit. As has been said,
the point of travelling is not
to arrive, but to return home
laden with pollen you shall work up
into the honey the mind feeds on.

What are our lives but harbours
we are continually setting out
from, airports at which we touch
down and remain in too briefly
to recognise what it is they remind
us of? And always in one
another we seek the proof
of experiences it would be worth dying for.

Surely there is a shirt of fire
this one wore, that is hung up now
like some rare fleece in the hall of heroes?
Surely these husbands and wives
have dipped their marriages in a fast
spring? Surely there exists somewhere,
as the justification for our looking for it,
the one light that can cast such shadows?

R. S. Thomas

Pilgrimages

There is an island there is no going
to but in a small boat the way
the saints went, travelling the gallery
of the frightened faces of
the long-drowned, munching the gravel
of its beaches. So I have gone

up the salt lane to the building
with the stone altar and the candles
gone out, and kneeled and lifted
my eyes to the furious gargoyle
of the owl that is like a god
gone small and resentful. There
is nobody in the stained window
of the sky now. Am I too late?
Were they too late also, those
first pilgrims? He is such a fast
God, always before us and
leaving as we arrive.
There are those here
not given to prayer, whose office
is the blank sea that they say daily.
What they listen to is not
hymns but the slow chemistry of the soil
that turns saints' bones to dust,
dust to an irritant of the nostril.

There is no time on this island.
The swinging pendulum of the tide
has no clock; the events
are dateless. These people are not
late or soon; they are just
here with only the one question
to ask, which life answers
by being in them. It is I
who ask. Was the pilgrimage
I made to come to my own
self, to learn that in times
like these and for one like me
God will never be plain and
out there, but dark rather and
inexplicable, as though he were in here?

R. S. Thomas

Áine agus Íde

Cad tá ort, a chailín, cén fáth an mí-shuaimhneas?
Tá tart orm, a mháithrín, sin fáth mo uaighnis.

Nár thugas duit bainne, is nach bhfuil tuilleadh ar fáil?
Thugais, a mháithrín, is bhíos buíoch é a fháil.

Tá uisce úr an tsléibhe anseo faoi do láimh!
Ní beag liom an t-uisce, a ghlaine is a cháil.

An mian leat fíon, a chailín chiúin óig?
Níl agat aon fhíon don íota seo am' dhó.

Cá raghair, a chailín, ní fhágair an baile?
Tá leanbh am iarraidh is téim dá· altrom.

Nach dána an mhaise dhuit a leithéid d'iontaibh!
Briathar an teachtaire a chuaidh fám' chroí.

Cad faoi do shláinte is an freastal gann seo?
Gealladh dom dáimh is uisce bithbheo.

An mbeidh aon trá, a iníon, ar fhlaithiúlacht do dhé bhig?
'Sé bhronn orm mo ghiniúin, mo bhás is m'aiséiri.

Áine, baindia na talún. Íde an daonnaí le tart mór is
máthair altrama na naomh.

Literally:

What is on you, girl, and why are you so uneasy?
I am thirsty, mother, that is why I am lonely.

Didn't I give you milk and isn't there more?
You did, mother and I was grateful to receive it.

There is water from the mountain here at hand!
I love water, so clear and fresh.

Do you want some wine, quiet young girl?
You have no wine for the thirst that burns me.

Where are you going, girl, will you leave the house?
A child is looking for me and I go to nurse him.

Isn't that bold of you, such confidence?
The word of the messenger went straight to my heart.

What of your health and the service without show?
I was promised affection and living water.

Will the generosity of your little hero ever run dry?
It is he who gave me my life, my death and my resurrection.

Áine, mother-earth, wonders at Íde's thirst and her faith in
Íosagán that calls her to be the foster-mother of the saints.

Micheál de Liostún

D: OTHER RESOURCES

Articles
The Holy Wells of Co. Kildare, Patricia Jackson in *Journal of Kildare Archaeological Society*. Volume 16 (1977- 1986)
The Holy Wells of County Dublin, Caoimhín Ó Danachair in *Reportum Novarum* – Dublin Diocese.

Books
A Pilgrim in Celtic Scotland
John J. Ó Ríordáin
The Columba Press 1997

A Walking Tour of Dublin Churches
Veritas 1988

An Introduction to Celtic Christianity
James P. Mackey
T. and T. Clark, Edinburgh 1989

Ancient Ireland. From prehistory to the Middle Ages
Jacqueline O Brien and Peter Harbison
Weidensfeld and Nicolson, London 1996

Archaeological Inventory of County Wicklow
Complied by Eoin Grogan and Annaba Klilfeather
Government Publications Office, Dublin

Celtic Fire. An Anthology of Celtic Christian Literature
Robert Van de Weyer
Darton Longman and Todd 1990

Celtic Miscellany
Kenneth Hurlstone Jackson
Penguin Books 1951

Celtic Spirituality
Post-Primary Diocesan Advisers, Dublin 1997

Celtic Worship through the Year
Ray Simpson
Hodder and Stoughton 1997

Bread of Tomorrow
Edited by Janet Morley
SPCK 1992

Dublin be Proud. A hundred years a growing
Pat Liddy
Chadworth Limited, Dublin 1987

Earth Prayers from Around the World
Edited by Elizabeth Roberts and Elias Amidon
HarperCollins 1991

Glendalough and Saint Kevin
Lennox Barrow
Dundalgan Press Ltd, Dundalk 1992

Glendalough. A Celtic Pilgrimage
Michael Rodgers and Marcus Losack
The Columba Press 1996

Guerrillas of Grace – Prayers for the Battle
Ted Loder
LuraMedia, San Diego California, USA 1984

Guide to the National Monuments of Ireland
Peter Harbison
Gill and Macmillian 1975

Image and Pilgrimage in Christian Culture. Anthropological Perspectives
Victor Turner and Edith L. B. Turner.
Columbia University Press, New York 1978

Irish Catholic Spirituality
John J. Ó Ríordáin
The Columba Press 1998

Irish Spirituality
Edited by Michael Maher
Veritas Publications 1981

Irish Poetry of Faith and Doubt. The Cold Heaven
Edited John F. Deane
Wolfhound Press 1991

Places of Pilgrimage
Bernard Jackson
Geoffrey Chapman 1989

Pilgrimage as Rite of Passage
A Guidebook for Youth Ministry
Robert J. Brancatelli
Paulist Press 1998

Pilgrimage in Ireland. The Monuments and the People
Peter Harbison.
Barrie and Jenkins Limited 1991

Psalm-Prayers for Every Mood
Kevin Lyon
The Columba Press 1996

Prayers for a Planetary Pilgrim
Edward M. Hays
Forest of Peace Books, Inc., KS 66048-0269, USA

Saint Patrick's World
Liam De Paor
Four Courts Press 1993

Sacred Places, Pilgrim Paths. An Anthology of Pilgrimage
Martin Robinson
HarperCollins 1997

Saltair: Prayers from the Irish Tradition
Pádraig Ó Fiannachta. Trans. Desmond Forristal
The Columba Press 1988

Seinn Alleluia 2000: Music for the Jubilee Year
Advisory Committee on Church Music
The Columba Press 1999

The Holy Wells of Ireland
Patrick Logan.
Colin Smythe Limited 1980 Reprinted 1992

The Iona Community Worship Book
Wild Goose Publications 1991

The Music of What Happens
John J. Ó Ríordáin
The Columba Press 1996

The Pleasures of Gaelic Poetry
Edited by Seán Mac Réamoinn
Allen Lane Penguin Books Ltd 1982

Towards a History of Irish Spirituality
Peter O'Dwyer
The Columba Press 1995

Wisdom of the Celtic Saints
Ed Sellner
Ave Maria Press, Indiana 1993

COPYRIGHT ACKNOWLEDGEMENTS

We gratefully acknowledge the following copyright permissions:

Three poems by Patrick Kavanagh by kind permission of the Trustees of the Estate of Patrick Kavanagh, c/o Peter Fallon, Literary Agent, Loughcrew, Oldcastle, Co Meath. The Dedalus Press for 'Seasons' by Paul Murray. Ateliers et Presses de Taizé, 71250 Taizé Community, France for four Taizé chants. Veritas Publications for a quotation from *Lighting the Shadows: Prayers and Reflections for Young People* by Donal Neary SJ. J. M. Dent & Sons for four poems by R. S. Thomas, from his *Collected Poems 1945-1990*. Faber and Faber Ltd for 'St Kevin and the Blackbird' by Séamus Heaney from his *The Spirit Level*. Críost 2000: The Kerry Jubilee Programme for Tomás Ó Caoimh's notes on St Kevin. Peter Harbison for a poem and permission to adapt a map of St Kevin's Way from his *Pilgrimage in Ireland*. NewStart 2000 Ltd and Churches Together in England for the 'Millennium Resolution'. GIA Publications Inc., Chicago, Illinois for 'Water of Life' by David Haas. Carcenet Press Ltd and David Higham Associates for 'Absence' by Elizabeth Jennings, from her *Collected Poems*. Brendan Kennelly and Bloodaxe Books for the poem 'Proof'. Cló na Cúirte Éigse for 'Áine agus Íde' by Micheál de Liostún. OCP Publications, Portland, Oregon, for 'We shall draw water joyfully' by Paul Inwood and for 'Be Not Afraid' by Bob Dufford SJ. 'How Lovely on the mountains are the feet of him. Our God Reigns' by Leonard E. Smith Jr, copyright © 1974 Kingsway's Thakyou Music, PO Box 75, Eastbourne, BN23 6NW, UK. The Word of God Music, administered by Copycare, PO Box 77, Hailsham, BN27 3EF, UK, for 'The Light of Christ' by Donal Fishel.